Visitors from the Stars

The Untold Story of UFOs

J.E.S.

Contents

Prologue

March 13, 1997. Phoenix, Arizona

THE BUSTLING CITY OF Phoenix is nestled beneath a vast desert sky; its streets are bright and hum with urban life. It was a night like any other in this modern city, but what would transpire over the next few hours would etch an unforgettable mark in the annals of UFO history.

As twilight turned to darkness, an eerie hush settled over the cityscape. Out of the dark expanse, an array of lights appeared in the sky, forming a distinct V-shape against the stars. The formation was massive, stretching over a mile wide, and it moved with a calculated precision that defied any scientific explanation.

Thousands of people from all walks of life stood in awe and fear as the V-shaped object glided silently across the sky. The lights looked like neither stars nor airplanes; they emitted an ethereal, phosphorescent glow that cast an otherworldly hue. Gasps of disbelief turned into whispers of astonishment as people tried to comprehend the inexplicable sight above them.

Tim Ley and his wife Bobbi, who had been out in their backyard, watched in awe as the strange formation passed overhead. At first, Tim dismissed it as a satellite or a passing airplane. Living near an airport, he had seen a lot of airplanes, so he was not perturbed at first. But as seconds turned into minutes, the lights began to defy all logic. Tim's voice trembled as he pointed to the formation of lights and said to Bobbi, with disbelief, "That's not something from here."

The object with the flashing lights was moving so slowly that it gave the appearance of a silent hovering object, which soon passed over their heads and went through between the tops of the mountain range towards Piestewa Peak in the direction of Phoenix Sky Harbor International Airport.

How could Tim know that this was merely the beginning? The sightings that would follow, the investigations that would span years, and the truths that would challenge the very logic or sense were not easy to come.

Newspaper offices and radio stations were inundated with phone calls from bewildered witnesses reporting the phenomenon. Police officers, firemen, and even pilots were among the crowd who stepped outside and witnessed this baffling spectacle. As the formation slowly disappeared beyond the horizon, a palpable sense of curiosity mixed with a touch of uneasiness lingered in the air.

In the days that followed, explanations ranging from secret aircraft and military maneuvers to weather anomalies were offered. Still, none could quell the overwhelming sense that something extraordinary had transpired that night. As the event would come to be known, the Phoenix Lights sparked debates, investigations, and a relentless search for answers that would persist for years to come.

This book sets out on a journey to educate and enlighten you about the puzzling world of Unidentified Flying Objects. Within its pages, you will discover the intriguing web of UFO sightings and encounters, warily setting up facts, speculative fiction, and even conspiracy theories and their coverups.

With a strong commitment to evidence-based analysis, it will unveil the historical chronology of these phenomena, tracing their evolution through different eras and cultural influences. The book asks for critical thinking, urging readers to assess claims with discerning eyes while adopting an environment of open-minded inquiry.

By presenting diverse perspectives from experts, scientists, skeptics, and diehard enthusiasts, it aspires to create a mosaic of viewpoints that challenges assumptions and broadens our understanding. Moreover, this book sheds light on the profound impact of UFO sightings on society, art, media, movies, literature, and the collective imagination of the masses. It provides a gateway to explore further this enduring mystery, inviting readers to embark on their personal exploration of this intricate but captivating subject.

Yes, UFOs are real in the sense that there have been numerous documented instances of objects flying in the sky that could not be immediately identified or explained. However, the term UFO does not necessarily imply that these objects are of extraterrestrial origin or have supernatural qualities. Instead, it simply signifies that the object observed is not readily identifiable based on available information and evidence. Many UFO reports can be attributed to conventional explanations once investigated thoroughly.

UFO sightings have been reported by people from various walks of life and across different parts of the world. These sightings often lead to speculation about their nature, including potential explanations such as misidentified aircraft, weather phenomena, atmospheric anomalies, secret military experiments, hoaxes, and much more.

In recent years, there has been increased attention on the subject of UFOs due to the release of previously classified government documents, the establishment of official investigation programs, claims by whistleblowers, and the acknowledgment by military and government officials of encounters with unidentified aerial objects. These developments have sparked debates about the potential implications of such encounters and the need for further research into understanding the nature of these phenomena.

The journey you are about to embark upon will unveil not only the mysteries of that particular night but also the vast number of UFO encounters that have captivated minds and ignited imaginations across the globe. The Phoenix Lights were just the beginning, a forerunner of the revelations, intrigues, and enigmas that lie ahead as we dig deep into the realm of the unexplained and the unearthly, beyond the stars and into the heart of a mystery that has tantalized minds for generations. The truth is out there, waiting to be discovered amidst the pages that lie ahead. Go ahead and read on.

Chapter 1

Architects from the Stars

IF YOU HAVE A curious interest in UFOs, one question that eventually will come to your mind is how long has this spectacle been going on? You will want to know what the earliest record of a UFO event reported is.

The Tulli Papyrus Scrolls

Once you start your research about UFOs, you will inevitably reach Tulli Scrolls. These scrolls relate to the Egyptian Pharaoh King Thutmose III, who reigned in Egypt from 1479 till 1425 BC.

So the story goes that in the late 1950s, Italian Egyptologist Alberto Tulli was wandering around in the labyrinth of Cairo's ancient bustling bazaar amidst the cacophony of sounds, colors, and aromas. The narrow alleys were alive, with merchants haggling over trinkets, spices, and carpets. Tulli had an insatiable curiosity and was always drawn to the mysteries of the past, and Cairo's bazaar seemed like the perfect place to discover such hidden treasures.

As he meandered through the winding paths, his eyes fell upon a dimly lit shop tucked away in a corner. The shop was filled with an eclectic mix of ancient artifacts, antique jewelry, and weathered papyrus scrolls that whispered stories of distant times. Tulli's heart quickened with excitement as he approached the dusty shop, feeling an inexplicable pull toward the treasures within.

Cairo Bazaar
(by Alex Alabache, Unsplash)

Among the artifacts, his gaze fixated on a collection of papyrus scrolls, their edges frayed and their surfaces bearing the marks of age. The merchant, an old man with wise eyes and a large flowing beard, noticed Tulli's interest and beckoned him closer. "Ah, esteemed visitor, you have an eye for the extraordinary," the merchant said with a warm smile. "These scrolls hold the secrets of civilizations long past."

Tulli's fingers traced the intricate patterns on the scrolls, his mind racing with wonder. He selected one particular papyrus scroll, its texture slightly rough under his touch. Unrolling it with care, he revealed a series of hieroglyphics, their meaning hidden beneath the ancient language.

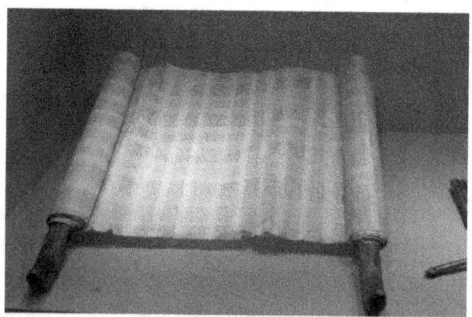

Ancient Scroll
(by Pexfuel)

The merchant's eyes twinkled as he spoke, his voice carrying the weight of ancient stories. "That, my friend, is a fragment of the ancient past. It has a tale woven by the hands of scribes from the time of the pharaohs. It speaks of an event that stirred the heavens and Earth alike".

Intrigued, Tulli leaned in, absorbing the merchant's words. He could barely decipher the hieroglyphics language. It seemed to say about a time when the fiery luminous discs flew over the skies. He could sense that the hieroglyphics painted a vivid picture of a civilization gripped by awe and uncertainty as the discs danced overhead in the sky, casting their brilliant glow upon the land.

Tulli's heart raced as he imagined the scene unfolding before his mind's eye. The ancient scribes' descriptions felt vivid, as if the events were unfolding in the present. Yet, his scholarly instincts held a hint of skepticism. Could this truly be an account of an encounter with beings from beyond, or was it a metaphorical tale of celestial wonders?

With a sense of determination, Tulli started to negotiate with the merchant and after a lengthy haggling session, which is a common ritual in these bazaars, and after consuming many rounds of black Arab coffee, he managed to strike a deal for what he thought was an outrageous sum of money. He reluctantly handed over the money to the bemused merchant, who said with a twinkle in his eye, "My friend, you have bought a treasure for mere pennies." The old merchant hurriedly packed the scrolls in a cotton wrap, worried that Tulli might change his mind. But Tulli was a happy man as the papyrus scrolls became his treasured possession, a mystery he carried with him to decipher later.

Back in his study in Rome, Tulli meticulously analyzed and translated the hieroglyphics, seeking to unravel the enigma of the text written on the scrolls. He consulted with fellow experts, debated with skeptics, and peered into old history books, looked at extinct language dictionaries. The more he studied, the more he realized that the ancient bazaar of Cairo had bestowed upon him a fragment of history that defied his expectations.

The papyrus scrolls were said to date back to the reign of Thutmose III, an ancient Egyptian pharaoh who ruled during the 15th century BC. According to Tulli, the papyrus contained a record of a strange event where 'fiery disks' were observed in the sky, emitting lights, sounds, and odor and displaying unusual behavior.

The text supposedly describes how the scribes of the pharaoh witnessed these phenomena and recorded them.

Here is how Tulli finally translated the text:

> "In the year 22 of the 3rd month of winter, sixth hour of the day... the scribes of the House of Life found there was a circle of fire that was coming in the sky... It had no head, the breath of its mouth had a foul odor. Its body one rod long and one rod wide. It had no voice. Their hearts became confused through it; then they laid themselves on their bellies... they went to the Pharaoh... to report it. His Majesty ordered... [an examination of] all which is written in the papyrus rolls of the House of Life. His Majesty was meditating upon what happened. Now after some days had passed, these things became more numerous in the skies than ever. They shone more in the sky than the brightness of the sun, and extended to the limits of four supports of the heavens... Powerful was the position of the fire circles. The army of the Pharaoh looked on with him in their midst. It was after supper. Thereupon, these fire circles ascended higher in the sky towards the south... The Pharaoh caused incense to be brought to make peace on the hearth... and what happened was ordered by the Pharaoh to be written in the annals of the House of Life... so that it be remembered forever."

It seems Tulli was seeing the first recorded history of UFO sightings. This was an incredible discovery, and as he told his peers about this discovery, it soon made him famous. The story of the Tulli Papyrus Scrolls, discovered in the bustling bazaars of Cairo, became the folklore of UFO stories forever.

However, skeptics say there are several reasons why the Tulli Papyrus Scrolls are considered to be a hoax. After the death of Tulli, the original papyrus scrolls were never found, and no other expert could examine them. The alleged discovery of this ancient Egyptian document by Alberto Tulli lacks credible historical records or primary sources supporting his existence and contributions to the field. The translated content of the papyrus itself, describing sightings of UFOs in ancient Egypt, exhibits linguistic inconsistencies and stylistic deviations from genuine ancient Egyptian texts.

Collectively, these reasons undermine the credibility of the Tulli Papyrus Scrolls, rendering it a widely recognized fabrication within the academic community. Still, enthusiasts consider it serious proof of alien visits by UFOs long past our times.

Did Starborn Architects Shape Our Past?

Our planet Earth has some amazing monuments constructed a long time ago. These constructions seem to defy the technological capabilities of their time either because they're too big, too heavy, or too complex. Some of the many grand monuments that dot the globe stand as a testament to humanity's audacious spirit, creativity, and hard labor.

As one gazes upon the monumental Pyramids of Egypt and ponders upon the celestial alignments of Stonehenge, their colossal stones dance with the heavens, and a tantalizing question lingers: Were these marvels truly fashioned by the hands of their times?

The Nazca Lines etched intricately across Peru's desert canvas, their scale evident only from the sky, beckon us to ponder the possibility of ancient earthlings gazing upward at the stars for inspiration. Teotihuacan's staggering symmetry and the Inca fortress Sacsayhuaman's colossal stones interlocked with a precision that defies explanation offer a provocative whisper from the past.

Could these monuments be the product of a connection beyond our understanding, guidance from the cosmos that ancient minds grasped more intimately than we dare imagine?

As we stand on the threshold of discovery of outer space and beyond, the echoes of the stars and the secrets of these stone enigmas continue to challenge our perceptions, inviting us to question the boundaries of human achievement in ages long past.

The Enigmatic Sentinals of the Desert

The Pyramids of Egypt constructed between 2550 and 2490 BC are a testament to ancient engineering mastery, rising with monumental grandeur on the desert landscape. The largest of the three, the Great Pyramid of Khufu, stands approximately 481 feet tall, a towering sentinel that held the title of the world's tallest structure for millennia. Its base covers an area of about 13 acres, with each side measuring around 756 feet.

What truly boggles the mind is the sheer scale of the construction. The Great Pyramid is estimated to consist of over 2.3 million stone blocks, with some of the largest individual stones weighing as much as 80 tons. These colossal blocks were quarried from nearby sites and hauled to the construction site, where they were meticulously carved, transported, and lifted into place.

The precision of the pyramid's construction, with its near-perfect alignment and arrangement of massive stones, remains a marvel of ancient engineering and architectural prowess. It's a humbling reminder of the civilization's dedication, ingenuity, and determination that orchestrated this monumental feat.

The idea that the Pyramids are considered proof of alien intervention is a popular but widely discredited theory within the realm of alternative history and pseudoscience. While some proponents of this theory point to certain aspects of the pyramids as evidence, it's important to note that the mainstream archaeological and historical consensus attributes the construction of the pyramids to ancient Egyptian civilizations, primarily during the Old and Middle Kingdoms.

Pyramids of Eqypt
(by Joshua Micheals, Unsplash)

The primary arguments used by proponents of the "alien intervention" argue that the precision with which the pyramids were constructed, aligning with cardinal points, and intricate stone-cutting techniques were beyond the capabilities of the people at that time; they must have required advanced extraterrestrial knowledge. They also say there is a lack of direct evidence, such as detailed hieroglyphics or inscriptions, explaining the techniques and methods used to construct the pyramids. They are amazed at the pyramids' layout and positioning, which exhibit alignments with certain celestial bodies or constellations that would have been challenging for ancient Egyptians to achieve without external guidance.

However, these arguments are countered by various well-established facts and evidence presented by experts. The Archaeologists say that tools, quarries, workshops, and even worker cemeteries support the idea that the ancient Egyptians had the skills, technology, and manpower to construct the pyramids. Although the pyramids themselves indeed lack detailed inscriptions, other ancient Egyptian texts and inscriptions provide insights into the construction techniques and methods employed.

They say that the construction of pyramids evolved, with earlier structures showing signs of experimentation and refinement that align with the gradual development of architectural and engineering knowledge. As far as alignment with celestial bodies is considered, they fit within the broader context of ancient Egyptian beliefs, culture, and architectural practices. They served as monumental tombs for pharaohs and were integral to the Egyptian concept of the afterlife.

While the idea of alien intervention in the construction of the pyramids might capture the imagination, it lacks empirical evidence and does not align with the established understanding of ancient Egyptian history, architecture, and culture. The mainstream consensus among historians, archaeologists, and experts is that the pyramids were built by skilled ancient Egyptian craftsmen and laborers using the knowledge and tools available at the time.

Celestial Connection in the Rocks

Experiencing Stonehenge at dawn during the solstice is a captivating experience. The solstices, occurring around June 21st and December 21st, mark the longest and shortest days of the year, respectively, and Stonehenge's alignment with the sun during these moments amplifies its enigmatic allure. The rising sun's alignment with the Heel Stone during the summer solstice and its connection to the setting sun during the winter solstice create a stunning visual spectacle.

Each year, on 21st June, a crowd of die-hard tourists and UFO enthusiasts at Stonehenge gather very early in the morning. As dawn breaks, the ancient stones gradually emerge from the darkness, enveloping the site in an ethereal ambiance of light and shadow. The sun rises behind the entrance to the stone circle, and rays of light are channeled into the center of the monument, causing a flash of light of enchanting beauty. The crowd erupts with vociferous shouts while utterly convinced that this is the work of some alien being.

This phenomenon is rather a testament to the remarkable understanding of astronomical events held by Stonehenge's builders, hinting at its profound cultural and spiritual significance. The experience offers a bridge between the past and present, inspiring a deep sense of wonder and connection to both the ancient world and the celestial rhythms that guided it.

Stonehenge
(by Mitch Hodge, Unsplash)

Stonehenge is a prehistoric monument located in Wiltshire, England. It consists of a ring of standing stones, each around 13 feet high, 7 feet wide, and weighing around 25 tons on average. The purpose and construction methods of Stonehenge have fascinated researchers and historians for centuries. While there is still some debate, it's generally believed that Stonehenge was built in several phases over centuries, starting around 3000 BC and continuing through 2000 BC. The monument's design evolved from a simple circular arrangement of holes and pits to the more complex structure we see today.

The first stones, the bluestones weighing around 4 tons each, were sourced from the only place in the UK where such stone exists, in the Preseli Hills in north Pembrokeshire in Wales, nearly 200 miles away. There is much archaeological debate surrounding the theories of how the stones got from Wales to Salisbury Plain.

A widely discussed hypothesis among academics proposes that these stones were extracted from a location in Wales, then transported mainly by water courses, and subsequently using log roller systems over land to reach the Stonehenge site. Despite ongoing efforts, no one has managed to recreate this achievement using the technologies available during that era. Additionally, no supporting evidence has been discovered along the presumed transportation route. Another prominent and potentially more credible theory suggests that the stones were naturally carried to Stonehenge by glaciers during the Ice Age.

The larger stones, known as Sarsen stones, originated from a site roughly 20 miles away. However, considering the absence of modern machinery and the pre-wheel era, this would have constituted a massive endeavor across uneven terrain. The Sarsens were likely roughly shaped at their source and then pulled atop tree trunks functioning as rollers all the way to Stonehenge. It's estimated that this monumental task would have required the efforts of up to a thousand laborers and might have taken over a decade to complete.

Stonehenge itself was constructed in a similar fashion as woodworking, with carefully carved joints and sockets in the stone to ensure precise fitting. Notably, Stonehenge's distinctiveness lies in its use of horizontal stones to create arches engineered to be flat despite the sloping terrain. The stones were also uniquely fashioned into blocks with flat sides. Given the absence of metal tools, shaping these immense stones using stone-on-stone techniques would have demanded extensive labor. Evidence of this labor-intensive process is apparent in the surrounding area, which is filled with stone chippings.

Raising the stones would have posed challenges without contemporary tools. Ditches were likely excavated to fit in the stones, with approximately one-third of the upright stones' lengths sunk below the ground level. The prevailing hypothesis suggests the construction of substantial earthen ramps over which the stones could be toppled into their designated holes. Then, using potentially rudimentary A-frames for leverage, the stones might have been pulled upright.

The exact purpose of Stonehenge remains a subject of speculation, as the people who built it left no written records. However, various theories suggest that it might have been used as a ceremonial or religious site, an astronomical observatory, a place for healing, or even a burial ground.

The alignment of the stones suggests a connection to astronomical events, particularly the solstices and equinoxes. Stonehenge's arrangement of massive standing stones has fueled speculation about extraterrestrial involvement. Some theories suggest that the stones were too heavy to be moved and set up by humans alone. However, archaeological research and experimentation have demonstrated that ancient people had the capability to quarry, transport, and erect these stones using simple tools and techniques.

Alien Signatures on Earth

The Nazca Lines are intricate geoglyphs etched into the desert floor, depicting various animals and shapes. Some UFO enthusiasts propose that these lines were created as landing strips or signals for aliens. Archaeologists, on the other hand, believe they were created by the Nazca culture for religious or ceremonial purposes.

Nazca Lines
(by Seiji Kapo, Unsplash)

Setting foot in the Nazca Desert, one is greeted by a landscape that appears deceptively unremarkable. The barren stretches of sand and rock seem indifferent to the secrets they hold beneath their surface. At the approach of the first designated viewing point for the Nazca Lines, squinting eyes and puzzled expressions are common as visitors strain to discern the enigmatic figures etched into the ground. One doesn't see much from there, but one has to go to a nearby airport and take an airplane ride for an amazing phenomenon to unfold.

Stepping onto the runway of the small Nazca airport, the true revelation begins. Boarding a small propeller aircraft specially designed for sightseeing, there is a feeling of anticipation building to a climax. As the propellers whir to life and the plane gains altitude, the world below transforms. The barren desert terrain takes on a new dimension as the lines come alive, revealing their intricate shapes and grandeur.

Peering out of the plane's window, one is immediately struck by the sheer scale of the geoglyphs. Etched into the ground with uncanny precision, the colossal figures stretch across the desert floor, each telling a unique story. The Monkey, the Hummingbird, the Spider, and other intricate designs suddenly come to life, painted on a canvas of sandy earth.

The airplane's altitude allows the opportunity to witness these figures in their entirety, a view that is impossible from the ground. The Nazca Lines' colossal size and precision become undeniable, defying explanation as they sprawl across the arid landscape, inspiring questions that seem to reverberate through time.

The Nazca Lines are an incredible testament to human ingenuity, artistry, and connection to the cosmos, that leave an indelible mark on even the crustiest tourist who thinks that he has seen it all. The journey from land to sky, from the routine to the extraordinary, shows that sometimes, to truly appreciate the grandeur of human achievement, one must soar above the clouds and look at history etched permanently on the face of the earth.

As the plane circles and banks, affording views of the Nazca Lines from various angles, a thought starts to crystallize in the visitor's mind: Could humans have really accomplished this monumental feat so long ago? The idea that the Nazca people meticulously etched these enormous figures into the ground seems almost implausible, especially when considering the limited technology they would have had at their disposal.

There are more than 800 straight lines, around 300 geometric shapes, and approximately 70 depictions of animals and plants, referred to as biomorphs. Certain straight lines extend up to a distance of 30 miles, whereas the biomorphs vary in length from 50 to 1200 feet.

They were made in the period of 800 BC to 650 AD and probably go back to the Paracas and Nazca people, lost cultures of Peru before the Inca period. Because there's so little rain, wind, and erosion, the exposed designs have stayed largely intact for 500 to 2000 years.

The Nazca drawings, believed to be up to two millennia old, continue to intrigue scientists due to their age, size, aerial visibility, and enigmatic nature. These designs, known as geoglyphs, were created by removing the upper layer of reddish rocks to reveal the contrasting white sandstone underneath.

However, understanding their purpose presents a more complex challenge. Initially explored in the early 1900s, these patterns were initially thought to align with celestial bodies or seasonal markers. Yet, more recent research proposes a connection between the Nazca lines and ceremonial or ritual sites associated with water and fertility.

Where No Man Has Gone Before

The appeal of the idea of extraterrestrial visitation to Earth is undeniable, especially in the context of humanity's rapid advancement in space exploration. As we set our sights on celestial bodies like the Moon, Mars, and even distant exoplanets, the notion that other intelligent beings might have already traversed the vast cosmic expanse to reach our planet captures our imagination.

This concept has been a cornerstone of science fiction literature, movies, and pop culture for decades, fueling discussions about the potential implications of contact with alien civilizations. Yet, while the idea sparks curiosity and wonder, it is crucial to emphasize that, despite widespread speculation and anecdotes, there is currently no concrete, scientifically verifiable evidence supporting the notion of past alien encounters on Earth.

In the absence of clear evidence, we must engage in rational and critical thinking when evaluating claims of extraterrestrial visitation. Human history is replete with remarkable accomplishments and extraordinary feats, often attributed to the resourcefulness, creativity, and ingenuity of ancient civilizations. Resorting to supernatural or extraterrestrial explanations for these magnificent structures can inadvertently diminish the intelligence and resourcefulness of our ancestors.

By studying the architectural and engineering methods employed by past societies, we gain insight into the incredible ways they harnessed the resources available to them and developed techniques that remain impressive even by today's standards.

These limitations of our current understanding do not negate the boundless potential for future discoveries in space. As humanity pushes the boundaries of space exploration and technology, we must remain open to the possibility of encountering alien life forms. However, grounding our speculations in scientific rigor and evidence is essential to distinguish between speculation and reality. As we venture further into the cosmos, let us carry the torch of rationality while nurturing the excitement and imagination that have always fueled our fascination with the unknown.

Chapter 2

The Aliens Are Here

THIS MIGHT LOOK LIKE a scene from the TV series The X-files: Sunday, Feb. 21, 2021, American Airlines flight 2292 was on a routine run from Cincinnati to Phoenix. The aircraft lined up on the runway and received the clearance to take off. The Captain looked at the first officer, and with a cocky smile, he said, "Let's roll on." He had done it hundreds of times. The aircraft lurched forward, and it was soon in the air.

The takeoff and the flight were uneventful, but when the plane was over the northeast corner of New Mexico west of Clayton, at an altitude of 37,000 feet, a strange event happened. The Captain inquired from the control tower, "Do you have any targets up here? We just had something go right over the top of us. I hate to say this, but it is like a long cylindrical object that almost looks like a cruise missile type of thing moving really fast right over on top of us". The pilot also double-checked his instruments; the TCAS (Traffic Collision Avoidance System) didn't indicate any warning. Everything else looked normal.

The FAA air traffic controllers scanned their radar scopes but did not find any flying object in the vicinity of the aircraft. The pilots, though slightly ruffled, carried on and landed the plane safely at Phoenix Airport. The authorities investigated the matter but were unable to explain what the missile-like object was.

It was not the first time a pilot had spotted an unexplained flying object while flying a commercial jet. In fact, it happens fairly regularly, and almost every time, they remain unexplainable. Some commercial pilots even avoid reporting them to escape getting a bad impression by the airlines.

In another recent incident, in July of 2022, Julious Figueroa, an ex-Navy pilot who now flies skydivers in Virginia, had a close encounter with a strange object while flying a plane carrying skydivers.

He claimed that while climbing at around 4,300 feet, he saw a spherical golden orb about the size of a small car and flying very fast. It approached his airplane and came to about 15 feet to his left, heading north. It started getting closer. Figueroa started turning the plane to the left. As the object passed by, swiftly missing his plane by a whisker, Figueroa let go a yell, which caused the people in the back of the plane to look out the window. Three of the skydivers saw it, too, including one of the instructors. By the time the plane turned a semi-circle, the object was already on the horizon and then vanished completely.

Figueroa contacted Air Traffic Control and asked if they had seen a drone on the radar, to which they said they didn't. He called again and described the object he saw and asked if they had seen it. There was a long pause on the other end, and then they said they didn't see anything on their radar.

Figueroa's narrative bears a striking resemblance to countless other encounters observed around the world. Presently, there is a surge of reports of Unidentified Flying Objects (UFOs) and Unidentified Aerial Phenomena (UAPs) coming from diverse locations.

The FOO Fighters

Nearing the conclusion of World War II, the members of the 415th Night Fighter Squadron found themselves confronted not with an ending but with what seemed like the start of a battle coming straight from the novel "War of the Worlds" by H.G. Wells.

The routine mission briefs of the 415th Night Fighter Squadron were taking a perplexing twist. Amidst accounts detailing aerial battles with the Luftwaffe across the Rhine Valley under German occupation, pilots started sharing accounts of mystifying luminous objects tailing their aircraft.

The most detailed report came from Lt. Fred Ringwald. He was flying as an observer in a night fighter under the command of pilot Lt. Ed Schlueter with Lt. Donald J. Meiers on the radar. It was a November night in 1944. The sky was peppered with scattered clouds, and a quarter moon cast a pale glow. Their flight path led them over the Rhine Valley just north of Strasbourg, straddling the French-German border.

Ringwald's voice broke the silence, uttering, "I find myself wondering about the nature of those lights over yonder, in the hills." Flying in a formation of eight to ten, these luminous objects emitted a burning orange glow, a scene that caught the attention of Lt. Ed Schlueter as he glanced out over his aircraft's right wing. Seeking confirmation through radio communication with Allied ground radar, their inquiries yielded in silence - no blip or no trace was detected.

Suspicion ran through their minds; could these fiery lights be a new secret German airborne weapon? Fuelled by this uncertainty, Lt.Schlueter, in a brave move, initiated a maneuver to confront the enigmatic lights, only to watch them dissolve into thin air, leaving him perplexed.

Initially worried about being ridiculed, the men avoided recounting their bizarre encounters. Yet, their experiences rippled through the ranks, causing amazement and apprehension among the flight crews.

Fast-forward to December 17, 1944, near Breisach, Germany, where a pilot was flying at a low altitude of approximately 800 feet. His eyes fixed upon a configuration of 5 or 6 lights alternating between vivid red and green hues, aligning in the distinct form of a 'T.' A peculiar dance unfolded as these lights followed his path, inching closer until they settled at an 8 o'clock position around 1,000 feet from his aircraft. And then, as swiftly as they had emerged, these lights dissolved, vanishing without a trace, leaving behind a trail of astonishment.

December 22nd, another event was reported. In proximity to Hagenau, a flight crew witnessed another extraordinary sight. A pair of radiant orbs surrounded by a large orange halo, seemingly emerging from the very earth itself, ascending majestically to an altitude of 10,000 feet. Maintaining a shadowy distance from the fighter for roughly two minutes, these lights then executed a graceful turn, veering off to a separate trajectory while flying at a level for several moments before flickering out of existence.

In the absence of any good name, the aviators gave these enigmatic lights the code name of: "foo fighters." The inspiration for this name came from the popular comic strip of the time "Smokey Stover," where the main character, a firefighter named Smokey, frequently quipped, "Where there's foo, there's fire."

The introduction of the foo-fighter phenomenon to the public came through a press reporter, who broke the news on 1st January 1945. Immediately, a large number of speculations surfaced regarding the origins of these peculiar lights. Some proposed that the sightings might be attributed to flares, weather balloons, or even St. Elmo's Fire, a phenomenon characterized by the glowing light at the extremities of aircraft amidst stormy weather.

However, the aircrew of the 415th Night Fighter Squadron dismissed these theories outright. The unique characteristics of these objects to track aircraft were different than the behavior of flares and weather balloons, while their experienced eyes could easily differentiate between the phenomenon of St. Elmo's Fire and the foo fighters.

An alternative perspective proposed that the airmen's accounts were the by-product of "combat fatigue," a euphemistic term implying that the stresses of warfare were inducing a state of mental instability. Yet, scant evidence substantiated this claim, as all the pilots were in good mental health.

The 415th Squadron boasted an otherwise impeccable service record, and when a correspondent from a popular magazine undertook the task of reporting on the squadron, it portrayed its members as wholly normal flyers. Their foremost preoccupation was combat, followed by interests in pin-up girls, poker, pastries, and wine.

Keith Krasney, son of Lt. Krasney, is keen to highlight that his late father did not conform to the archetype of a UFO enthusiast. Strikingly, he never advanced the notion that the luminous, wingless, cigar-shaped entity that glided alongside his aircraft was of extra-terrestrial origin.

Characterizing his father as pragmatic and analytical, Krasney Jr. reveals that his father meticulously documented his foo-fighter sighting, supplementing his notes with illustrative sketches in a personal notebook.

Despite his absence of inclination towards conspiracy theories, Keith Krasney acknowledges that his father harbored a single speculative notion: the possibility that the phenomenon stemmed from cutting-edge secret German technology launched in the waning stages of the war.

Various groups, amateur psychologists, enthusiasts of military aviation, and proponents of conspiracy theories endeavored to offer explanations. However, none felt as credible within the airmen's collective assessment. The notion of hallucinations induced by battle fatigue was discarded, as was the idea that the lights might emanate from remotely guided clandestine German weaponry, given the absence of any destructive repercussions. The theory of St. Elmo's fire, a luminous discharge resulting from the interaction of electrical fields with pointed objects, appeared implausible due to the foo fighters' remarkable agility.

The Army Air Command eventually dispatched officers to probe the matter, although the findings of their investigation were lost in the aftermath of the war. The year 1953 witnessed the CIA convening a panel of distinguished scientists, experts in experimental aviation technology, to evaluate whether the lights posed a threat to national security. Known as the Robertson Panel, chaired by Caltech physicist Howard P. Robertson, this group did not furnish an official verdict.

Historian Ziebart offers a strange insight. He thinks that the foo fighters might have eluded radar detection because they constituted mere luminous emanations. Traditional radar requires solid entities for detection; thus, if any airborne anomalies existed, the pilots would undoubtedly see them, even though they not be detected by radar.

Several prevailing theories have sought to explain the enigma of the foo fighters, ranging from the straightforward proposition that they might be extraterrestrial spacecraft, to the possibility of being meteorological phenomena such as ball lightning.

The CIA's dismissal of foo fighters as 'electromagnetic' occurrences adds another layer of intrigue, while the possibility of sunlight reflecting off ice crystals presents an alternative perspective.

The conjecture that their prevalence during World War II could hint at their origins as experimental German technology adds historical intrigue, and the notion of visual hallucinations experienced by pilots during nocturnal flights also emerges as a plausible explanation.

The Flying Saucer is Born

We will never know exactly what private pilot Kenneth A. Arnold saw 75 years ago on June 24, 1947, while flying near Mount Rainier. What he said he saw and spent the rest of his life trying to explain is baffling He introduced the words "flying saucer" to the vocabularies of millions of people around the world which perhaps had an even greater historical impact than the sighting itself.

It was his description of the object flying as if it were "saucers skipping over water" that steered the reporters to coin the term "flying saucer." The strange part of the story is that Arnold never described the object as saucer or disc-shaped. He described them as crescent-shaped similar to swallow wings.

As the story goes Arnold took off on CallAir A-2, a single-engine light airplane from Chehalis Airfield in Washington. He had planned to go to attend an air show in Pendleton, Oregon. His flight plan included a refueling stop at Yakima, Washington. He was no novice, with 4,000 hours of flying time under his belt he was an expert pilot. He was also a volunteer of an Idaho search and rescue unit. The skies were clear and the winds light. He decided to take a detour from his original flight plan for a particular purpose.

He was aware that a Curtiss C-46 Commando transport with 32 Marines on board had crashed along his flight path and Arnold hoped to find the wreckage of the downed aircraft and claim a $5,000 reward.

At about 3:00 p.m., while Arnold circled his aircraft around 20 miles west of Mt. Rainier in search of the C-46 plane, he noticed a sudden bright flash coming from the northeast. He was taken aback, assuming it might be a military pilot flying a shiny P-51 plane, catching the sun's reflection on the wings.

As more flashes followed, Arnold dismissed the possibility of the nearby flying Douglas DC-4 airliner causing them. He stated that these flashes were originating from nine gleaming objects flying in a staggered formation, stretching about five miles in length. Arnold described these objects as circular, approximately 100 feet in diameter, and lacking any discernible tails. These objects exhibited periodic flipping, banking, and weaving from side to side, resembling the movements of a Chinese kite's tail.

The formation of objects was passing in front of Arnold, prompting him to time their journey from Mt. Rainier to Mt. Adams. Based on his calculations, he estimated that these objects were moving at a speed of around 1,200 mph, twice the speed of any known airplanes existing during that time. It would take several months before Col. Chuck Yeager piloted the Bell X-1 rocket aircraft to a speed of 700 miles per hour, breaking the sound barrier.

Arnold strongly refuted claims that he had initially used the term "flying saucers" to describe the objects. However, an article by Megan Garber published on June 15, 2014, in The Atlantic attributed Arnold to using the phrases "saucer," "disk," and "pie-pan" in his depiction of the observed objects. The day after the sighting, Arnold recounted his experience to press reporters of an Oregonian newspaper. The article printed in the next day's paper used the term "saucer-like aircraft."

Arnold knew that a news story about the sighting would provoke comments from the military. A brief article was published in the press, and the article used the phrase "nine bright saucer-like objects" to describe what Arnold had reported seeing. By afternoon, the narrative of "flying saucers" rapidly spread across the nation.

During a radio interview with Arnold on June 26, the host noted the speed at which the story engulfed the country. It was covered in every news broadcast, aired on the radio, and featured in every newspaper in the country. A newspaper ran a headline reading, "Supersonic Flying Saucers Spotted by Idaho Pilot." Arnold became a sensation in the media, although he did not welcome the spotlight. Reflecting on the situation three decades later, Arnold commented, "I have naturally faced some awkward moments now and then due to misquotes and misinformation" that was printed in various publications.

Over time, Arnold's description of the sighting underwent many changes. In a report sent to the U.S. Air Force in July, Arnold depicted a shape resembling the back of a shoe, with a rounded leading edge and a tapering trailing edge. A similar form can be seen in the Vought V-173 Flying Pancake, an aircraft at the National Air and Space Museum. This aircraft is yellow, disk-shaped, and features two propellers on one side and two wings on the other. The Flying Pancake lacks a traditional fuselage, with its broad, narrow, low-aspect-ratio wing encompassing the cockpit and twin engines.

There were various reports of Unidentified Flying Objects (UFOs) dating back centuries before the mid-1940s, but World War II signaled a new era of interest. Kenneth Arnold's momentous sighting in 1947, along with a widely publicized UFO event near Roswell, New Mexico, later that summer, played a significant role in intensifying the fascination with extraterrestrial visitors and establishing an entirely new subculture known as "ufology."

Although Arnold is credited with the sighting of the nine flying objects, he wasn't the only one who claimed to have seen the UFOs on that day. There were two other reports of presumably the same incident.

Arnold's story was corroborated by a newspaper, which reported that two other persons also observed the nine shiny objects in the sky. One of the people in Oklahoma City described it as a large, shiny, silver-colored object that was flying very fast.

Another man in Kansas City, Missouri, saw multiple objects and described them that they were flying so fast he could not count their numbers before they vanished, leaving vapor trails.

These sightings confirmed that Arnold saw the objects. However, even today, the observation of Kenneth Arnold remains unexplained. But the words "flying saucer" became a standard term for all kinds of UFOs in popular literature forever.

Autopsy of an Alien

On July 8, 1947, Roswell Army Air Base, located in Roswell, New Mexico, released a press statement indicating the recovery of a wreckage from a crashed flying saucer. However, a few days later, the base retracted its initial statement, asserting that the recovered materials were merely debris from a weather balloon. The Roswell incident, however, lost public attention for several decades until the rise of UFO conspiracy theories many years later.

Shockingly, in 1978, a retiring intelligence officer of the Roswell base appeared on television to confirm that the initial statement from the military about the Rosewell incident had indeed been true. After this revelation, the incident became a prominent topic of discussion. In the United Kingdom, a private TV channel broadcast a documentary featuring fresh evidence related to the Roswell incident. Among the compelling evidence was previously unreleased graphic and chilling footage that depicts an autopsy conducted on extraterrestrial beings recovered from the crash site.

In this film, the focus was on the post-mortem examination being carried out on the alien. The creature's unclothed body is stretched out on a dissecting table equipped with drainage tubes for blood. Medical professionals in white lab coats are observed attending to the body, tilting the head, and probing a substantial wound on the alien's leg. Even the alien's six toes are meticulously shown.

The autopsy sequence advances, featuring the opening of the chest cavity to remove internal organs, followed by the sawing of the skull to extract the brain. Throughout the autopsy, the clock's hands slowly progress from ten to eleven, indicating an hour-long procedure. However, the grainy, silent film footage was full of inconsistencies.

But whose body is the subject of investigation in this case? The Roswell alien garnered crazy attention due to its lack of identifiable genitalia, which could imply a default female classification. Throughout history, there has been a recurring theme of monstrous creatures representing male anxieties about the female body and sexuality.

The scrutiny and perceived punishment of the Roswell alien's body can be seen as a classic example of voyeuristic fantasy.

The alien's body appears more androgynous than distinctly female. In the footage, medical professionals extract portions of the alien's eyes and scrutinize its pelvic region in an attempt to determine its sexual characteristics.

Ultimately, the Roswell footage raises the question of whether it is authentic or fabricated. What is the actual truth? During a TV program, one of the interviewees recounted the threats she faced as a child to coerce her into 'forgetting' what she had witnessed. Her emotionally charged narrative resembled that of an abuse survivor sharing her story after years of silence.

The Roswell incident has become a substantial source of fascination for those interested in UFOs in both the United States and other countries. This interview and subsequent autopsy footage resulted in a resurgence of interest in UFOs and the rise of anti-government conspiracy theories.

Although the film footage and the interviews have been debunked many times by various agencies and investigative reporters, they still remain part of the UFO folklore.

Chapter 3

Alien Abductions

THIS IS ONE OF the most remarkable cases of alien abduction, and it holds a prominent place in the UFO files, primarily because it was the first abduction case that caught the attention of UFO researchers and the government.

This incident also prompted the US Air Force to intensively and covertly investigate the abduction phenomenon, but they kept the results of their investigation mostly under wraps.

Betty and Barney Hill Abduction

On the night of September 19, 1961, a couple named Betty and Barney Hill experienced a life-changing event while driving back from a vacation in Canada. The incident occurred near Lancaster, New Hampshire, as they spotted a brightly lit object in the sky that was distinctly different from any regular aircraft or helicopter.

Filled with a mix of anxiety and curiosity, they pulled over at a picnic area near Twin Mountains to observe the object through binoculars. The craft had unusual features, including porthole-like windows. Betty and Barney were both captivated by the extraordinary nature of the object, and they couldn't help but consider the possibility of UFOs and extraterrestrial beings. The encounter left them filled with both euphoria and anxiety, setting the stage for a significant turn in their lives.

Approaching Franconia Notch in the White Mountain National Forest, Betty and Barney Hill had a closer encounter with the craft. The object moved silently and performed remarkable maneuvers above the forest, even briefly hovering and displaying small wings. As the craft seemed about to land, strange buzzing sounds emanated from it, causing Barney to fear a collision. He stopped the car and observed the craft hovering just above them.

Barney cautiously came out of the car, armed with his loaded pistol, and saw humanoid figures with penetrating eyes and dressed in black clothing observing him through the craft's windows. One of them communicated a mental command for him to stay and watch. Fearful of the consequences, Barney obeyed and continued watching. Worried about their safety, he returned to the car, started the engine, and drove away quickly, fearing capture by the beings. But the craft disappeared, bringing reprieve to the Hills.

As they continued their journey back home, Betty and Barney Hill wondered about the extraordinary encounter they had experienced, speculating about the nature of the unidentified craft. Despite their excitement, they felt disturbed by the encounter for reasons they couldn't quite understand. The encounter left them shaken, but they managed to escape the unsettling situation, apparently unharmed. Or were they?

Upon returning home, they realized, to their shock, that a chunk of time during their drive was unaccounted for, and memories of this period were wiped out. Additionally, they noticed many physical anomalies. Barney's binoculars strap and shoes were torn, Betty's dress was ripped, and both of their watches malfunctioned and did not work. There seemed to be more to the incident, but their full recollection of the event remained elusive to them.

In the following days and weeks, Betty and Barney Hill experienced distressing nightmares that led them to uncover the disturbing truth of their encounter. Unsettling images were slowly emerging in their dreams in the days ahead. The dreams depicted the UFO landing near them and the crew taking control of them, guiding them onto the craft.

The encounter turned darker as both were subjected to strange experiments. Betty had an unexplained device inserted into her navel, while Barney was manipulated to ejaculate. These images strongly hinted at an extraterrestrial program linked to human reproduction, casting the Hills as prisoners of alien beings.

The dreams unveiled a more complex narrative than the Hills had initially understood. It seemed likely that they had been taken aboard an alien spacecraft and subjected to traumatic and bizarre experiments. The enigmatic creatures behind their ordeal treated them as mere subjects for experimentation, with the Hills only gradually realizing their role as unwitting test subjects.

Betty and Barney endured the distressing aftermath of their encounter for approximately two years. In 1963, seeking resolution, they turned to Dr. Benjamin Simon, a skilled Boston psychiatrist who specialized in hypnosis. Recognizing that much was hidden within their subconscious, Dr. Simon aimed to uncover these buried memories.

The complexities of the human mind often lead to suppression of fear-inducing experiences, but in the Hills' case, it appeared there was intentional manipulation of their memories. Dr. Simon's work unveiled that while the couple couldn't consciously remember the events, they retained vague memories within their dreams.

As the hypnosis sessions progressed, a comprehensive story emerged: a narrative of complete alien abduction, lost time, and disturbing experiments. These events were manipulated by alien creatures from an unidentified world.

The story of Betty and Barney Hill's encounter gained significant public interest, leading to their public lectures and the publication of a book titled "The Interrupted Journey" in 1966, authored by John Fuller and with their permission. The book became widely popular in both the UFO research community and among the general public.

Soon after their encounter, Betty contacted Pease Air Force Base to share their experience, and she spoke to Major Paul W. Henderson, who prepared a detailed investigative report on the incident.

Barney and Betty continued to lead their quasi-normal lives after that fateful encounter. However, Barney struggled with the trauma from the encounter, leading to gradually worsening health issues. He passed away at the age of forty-six in 1969, while Betty remained healthy and active in UFO circles until she died in 2004 at the age of eighty-five.

Although the abduction of Betty and Barney Hill became the world's most famous alien abduction of all time, even rudimentary research on the topic will yield case after case demonstrating how and why government agencies believe that the alien abduction phenomenon is real and that they are watching it seriously.

... and there are more

A very large number of alien abduction cases have been reported. Surely some are hoaxes, pranks, and attention-getting dramas, and some are to gain monetary benefits. But however implausible they seem to be, in many cases, it is apparent that the victim is speaking the truth, and most of the account comes while they are under hypnosis under medical supervision -- which makes us wonder, is it really happening?

Judy Doraty

This is also one of the most peculiar stories of alien abduction, providing insights into the motives behind alien actions. It answers some of the questions about why the aliens are doing it all.

On the night of May 23, 1973, Judy Doraty spotted a disk-shaped craft while driving near Houston, Texas. It appeared as a large, bright light in the sky that caught her attention. As she drove along, she noticed the light seemed to be following her car. Initially, she speculated it might be a helicopter bound for Galveston's airport, but closer observation revealed it to be a unique flying vehicle, unlike anything she'd ever seen.

Approaching near a farmland, she pulled over and got out of her car. The object continued to follow her movements, eventually approaching much closer. To her astonishment, the bright light transformed into a massive, silent, circular craft gliding over the fields. While she was puzzling over it, in a matter of seconds, it shot vertically upwards into the sky and disappeared.

Judy assumed the encounter had ended and returned to her car to safely drive home. However, in the days following this close encounter, she gradually realized that there was more to the experience than she initially remembered. Recurring vivid dreams, escalating into nightmares, began haunting her. These nightmares contained terrifying images of UFOs and aliens, though they remained confusing and fragmented.

During these dreams, Judy became aware of a "missing time" period in her recollections. Evidently, the aliens had attempted to erase her memory to prevent disclosure of the encounter. For years, she endured debilitating headaches and distressing nightmares, which she suffered in silence.

Eventually, she sought psychiatric and medical help. During her examination under hypnosis by Dr. Leo Sprinkle, a specialist in such matters, Judy managed to recall some of the missing memories. During this hypnotic state, she recollected moments of the encounter that had been erased from her conscious memory. She remembered stepping out of her car and witnessing a peculiar spotlight piercing the darkness. This light appeared to possess a tangible quality, and suddenly, it grabbed and lifted a struggling calf from the field into the air.

Curiously, she seemed to remember from being near the craft to being on board. She recalled strange simultaneous experiences. During her abduction, she sensed aliens were using medical instruments to examine her. She also observed the calf being taken onto the craft and then dissected systematically, and then it was dropped from a height to the ground with a thud. Faint recollections emerged of her daughter also being abducted and examined by the aliens.

The aliens seemed to pick up on her distress and provided an explanation. They told her they were conducting tests on all life forms on Earth. According to them, they had been observing Earth for a long time, examining everything from the air, soil, plant life, and fauna. Their goal was to comprehend the planet's workings. They felt alarmed by the loss of life due to pollution and wars and expressed their concerns.

The Air Force Office of Special Investigations (AFOSI) at Kirtland Air Force Base in New Mexico became involved and created a classified file on

Judy Doraty's experience. AFOSI found her abduction, coupled with the cattle mutilation incident and the aliens' interest in worldly matters, quite baffling but offered no explanation.

Charles Hickson and Calvin Parker Jr.

On the night of October 11, 1973, Charles Hickson and Calvin Parker Jr. arrived at the sheriff's office in Pascagoula, Mississippi, in a state of panic, speaking incoherently. They were claiming that they had just been abducted by aliens from the banks of the Pascagoula River. On examination, both men had needle puncture marks on their arms.

Initially, sheriff's investigators were skeptical, suspecting that the men were intoxicated or simply lying to get attention. Yet, after conducting interviews and secretly recording the men's conversation, hoping to unveil a hoax, they found Hickson and Parker consistently talking about their encounter with the aliens, showing fear and anxiety. Subsequently, both men underwent polygraph tests, which they passed.

They had gone on a fishing trip that evening on the river, where they remained until sunset. Hickson recalled the incident, "I was just about to get more bait when I heard a strange zipping sound. I looked up and saw a blue flashing light. Calvin turned around as well. There it was, a 30-foot-long object with a small dome on top, an unidentified flying object with pulsating blue lights moving along the Pascagoula River."

The authorities later sent them for further medical examination, and under hypnosis, they said that the craft hovered slightly above the ground, and three smaller entities emerged, hovering alongside it. The men experienced sudden paralysis as the creatures gripped them with their "lobster-like claws," goaded them towards their vessel, and finally took them aboard the craft. Inside the craft, Hickson recalled enduring a physical examination by a "large eye" accompanied by a constant mechanical buzzing sound.

Afterward, they were returned to the river bank from the same place where they were picked up. Apparently, their ordeal was over. Gathering their wits, Parker raised his arms and started screaming, seeking help urgently.

News of the incident spread rapidly, attracting national attention. Skeptics dismissed the story, attributing it to sleep paralysis and suggestibility, while UFO enthusiasts validated their claims. Pascagoula became a hub for believers who camped out in foil-covered attire, anticipating contact with extraterrestrial visitors, but without success.

Hickson remained a respected figure in the community, embraced the media attention, sharing his account with anyone interested. But Parker told the media that he had blacked out during the incident and couldn't recall the events.

Despite his statement, Parker did recollect the encounter, fearing he had been exposed to something harmful. After returning home from the sheriff's department, he even bathed in bleach. Within weeks, he left town, eventually marrying and finding work in the oil fields, promising himself quitting if recognized and leading a quiet life.

Hickson passed away in 2011, while Parker, now in his 60s, gradually reemerged from seclusion and, in 2018, published a book detailing his traumatic experience.

Myrna Hansen

On May 5, 1980, Myrna Hansen encountered an otherworldly event while driving to Eagle's Nest, New Mexico, after a trip to Oklahoma. Her experience matches the classic pattern of an alien abduction.

During their trip, Myrna and her six-year-old son reached the vicinity of Cimarron when they spotted several strange crafts over a nearby field. Both mother and son watched in shock as one of these crafts deployed a powerful light, what could be called a "tractor beam," to lift a grazing cow from the field and onto the craft. The crafts swiftly vanished, and the duo returned to their car unscathed.

Subsequent medical intervention and hypnosis sessions unveiled the true sequence of events that transpired that evening. Shortly after the initial sighting, both Myrna and her son found themselves taken aboard one of the crafts in a manner similar to the cow. The aliens responsible for this abduction resembled the commonly described "gray" aliens. Stripped of their clothing, both mother and son underwent various examinations and procedures conducted in a clinical and calculated manner.

During the course of events, they inadvertently witnessed the surgical procedures being performed on the captured cow. Upon seeing her distress, the alien informed Myrna that it was necessary without further explanation.

Additionally, Myrna recalled encountering a tall figure with a "jaundiced color" who told her that their abduction was a mistake that shouldn't have occurred. This enigmatic figure was dressed in attire resembling that of a priest. Yet, the unfolding events were far from over and were about to escalate into an even more bizarre ordeal.

The craft with them on board ultimately landed in the deserts of New Mexico, and Myrna and her son were led to an underground facility hidden within the expansive mountain ranges of the region. Within the base, they observed more gray aliens engaged in various tasks. Amazingly, they also encountered ordinary humans working alongside these alien creatures.

At this point, Myrna's son was separated from her, causing her to panic. She attempted to escape her captors, frantically calling her son's name. In her haste, she stumbled upon a dimly lit room containing large vats and illuminated containers. To her horror, one vat held a bubbling liquid that contained suspended human body parts. The shock overwhelmed her, and she collapsed to the floor, unable to comprehend the monstrous scene before her.

Subsequently, her captors took her to another room and implanted sophisticated tracking devices into her body. Her son was then reunited with her. Both were subjected to intense flashes of light in an apparent attempt to erase their memories of the encounter. Following this ordeal, they were taken to a craft similar to the one that initially abducted them and transported back to their car. Myrna drove home without any further incident.

Remarkably, Air Force officials acknowledged that Myrna's descriptions under hypnosis matched with a classified area of the base known as the 'Manzano Weapons Storage Complex,' an underground facility, which was totally out of bounds for civilians. This unexpected corroboration added credibility to her astonishing account.

Cattle Mutilations

In 1973, unusual occurrences began in Iowa, prompting concerned farmers to notify local law enforcement of unsettling incidents. They reported discovering many of their cattle dead in the fields without any explainable reason. The manner of these cattle deaths baffled ranchers – their eyes, ears, tongues, anuses, udders, and sex organs had been surgically removed with precision, seemingly using sharp instruments. Additionally, the animals' carcasses had been drained of blood. Notably, no tracks or footprints were found nearby, and the typical scavengers were conspicuously absent.

Between April and October of 1975, around 200 cases of cattle mutilation were documented in Colorado to become a recognized national concern. Throughout the 1970s, incidents of this nature escalated across the American heartland.

Finally, in 1979, the FBI launched an investigation into a series of such occurrences reported on New Mexico's Indian lands. By then, thousands of cattle mutilations had been reported, resulting in substantial financial losses for livestock owners.

These deaths were far from ordinary. The cows displayed missing genitals and eyeballs, with their skin seemingly subjected to high-temperature devices, possibly laser-based tools. Unlike the savage aftermath left by coyote attacks, these mutilations featured meticulously precise incisions.

In Colorado, investigations uncovered two suspected aircraft landings near dead cattle, marked by three triangular pod impressions. These impressions, 14 inches in diameter, were accompanied by smaller triangular tripods.

The cow's foottracks indicated its struggle and fall, surrounded by the smaller tripod tracks. The grass along the path of the tripods appeared scorched, and a peculiar yellow oily substance was found beneath two of the small tripods. Laboratory tests were unable to identify its content, as it seemingly dissolved or disintegrated during testing.

Two primary viewpoints emerged regarding cattle mutilations: one group considered them unexplained phenomena, while the other attributed them to ordinary cattle deaths misrepresented as paranormal occurrences. Those advocating for the unexplained theory held varying opinions on the possible causes. Some law enforcement circles speculated that the mutilations might be connected to peculiar quasi-religious rituals or even Satanists.

Ultimately, the FBI's investigation debunked the notion of an enigmatic force at play. On January 15, 1980, the Bureau concluded the investigation, releasing a statement asserting that "none of the reported cases has involved what appear to be mutilations by other than common predators."

A Government Cover-up?

The concept of alien abductions is a controversial topic, to say the least, but definitely sensational. While some people believe these accounts are genuine experiences, others view them as products of psychological factors, sleep paralysis, or other explanations.

The government's involvement in alleged alien abductions is less commonly discussed compared to UFO sightings. Some conspiracy theories suggest that the government is aware of alien abductions and might be monitoring them.

The conspiracy theories further claim that not only government is actively suppressing information, but they may be collaborating with extraterrestrial beings and concealing evidence of abductions to avoid panic in the public. Still, such theories often rely on anecdotal accounts and lack substantial proof.

Chapter 4

Unexplained Evidence

As EARLY AS 1973, Steven Spielberg was planning his next film, a science fiction movie in which the humans are shown to come in contact with aliens. He wanted a unique and captivating title for the movie.

And guess where he turned to get his title for the movie, "The Blue Book Project," an Air Force dossier that recorded all UFO/Alien events. This project had J. Allen Hynek, an astronomer and UFO researcher, as a consultant to the government.

Hynek divided alien encounters into different classes based on the nature of the interaction between humans and the aliens.

Under Hynek's classification system were:

1. Close Encounters of the First Kind: *Visual sightings of a UFO.*

2. Close Encounters of the Second Kind: *Visual sightings of a UFO with physical evidence, such as marks on the ground or damage to vegetation.*

3. Close Encounters of the Third Kind: *Sightings of UFOs that involve direct interaction with the aliens.*

Spielberg was fascinated by the idea of these different levels of encounters and their potential for storytelling in the movie. He used this classification system as a foundation for his film's narrative.

Of course, Spielberg chose the movie title "Close Encounters of the Third Kind," which signifies the most profound and direct form of contact between humans and extraterrestrial beings, which is a central theme of the movie.

The movie, released in 1977, was a box office hit, and this title phrase gained immense popularity through its portrayal by the movie's imaginative depiction of these encounters. This led to this phrase becoming part of popular culture.

Whistleblower Alleges Government Cover-Up

In July 2023, during a House Oversight Committee hearing, David Grusch, a former national reconnaissance officer of the UAP Task Force at the U.S. Department of Defense, provided startling testimony.

He claimed that the U.S. government had concealed evidence of extraterrestrial life for an extended period. Grusch, acting as a whistleblower, asserted that the government had possession of crashed unidentified vehicles and biological remains suspected to be of non-human origin but never revealed it.

Grusch further disclosed that while fulfilling his official duties, he learned about a secretive UAP (Unidentified Anomalous Phenomena) crash retrieval and reverse engineering program. However, he was denied access to this program.

He underlined that his testimony was based on information conveyed to him by individuals with established credibility and dedicated service to the nation. Many of these individuals provided substantiating evidence, including photographs, official documents, and classified oral accounts.

Grusch contended that military resources earmarked for other initiatives were diverted to attempt the reverse engineering of certain purportedly non-human technologies.

However, despite the hearing, conclusive proof of extraterrestrial life remained elusive. Grusch clarified that he hadn't personally witnessed any UFOs and declined to share specific details of his claims openly, citing reasons of security. Nevertheless, he expressed his willingness to provide more comprehensive information in a closed-door session.

How to Keep Track of it All?

Here's a timeline of how much the government knew and how much they let the public know what was happening out there.

1947-1969: Project Blue Book

Project Blue Book was a program conducted by the United States Air Force that aimed to study and investigate Unidentified Flying Objects (UFOs). The program was officially known as the United States Air Force UFO Research Program and was active from 1952 to 1969.

Project Blue Book had a dual set of objectives, each serving a distinct purpose. The foremost goal was to meticulously assess whether Unidentified Flying Objects (UFOs) presented a potential security threat to the United States. Secondly, the project aimed to ascertain whether UFOs contained any unique scientific insights or advanced technological elements that had the potential to contribute significantly to scientific and technical advancement.

As this project unfolded, it embarked on a comprehensive journey to fulfill these intertwined aims. By thorough investigation and analysis, Project Blue Book sought to shed light on the possible implications of UFOs for national security, acknowledging the potential impact on the safety of the nation.

The project undertook a rigorous examination of UFOs, aiming to discern any distinctive attributes that could potentially offer groundbreaking insights into science and technology. This pursuit of knowledge was rooted in the belief that UFOs, if found to possess novel properties or technological prowess, could enrich ongoing scientific and technical endeavors.

Project Blue Book collected and examined thousands of UFO reports and sightings from across the United States and around the world. The program employed various methods to investigate these reports, including interviews with witnesses, analysis of photographic evidence, and consultations with experts in fields such as astronomy, meteorology, and psychology. The program's findings were then used to generate reports and conclusions about the nature of the reported sightings.

Over the years, the majority of the cases were eventually identified as misidentifications of natural phenomena, aircraft, weather balloons, and other explainable events. However, a small percentage of cases remained unexplained despite the thorough investigations.

Project Blue Book's final report, officially titled "Project Blue Book - Special Report No. 14," was published in 1955. In two decades, the U.S. Air Force cataloged and contained a statistical analysis of over 12,618 sightings of UFOs as part of this project.

Special Report No. 14 concluded that about 22% of the cases were categorized as "unidentified," meaning that after thorough investigation, these cases remained unexplained. However, the term "unidentified" in this context doesn't necessarily mean evidence of extraterrestrial activity; it simply indicates that the specific cause of these sightings could not be definitively determined.

The final verdict of Project Blue Book regarding UFOs was that the vast majority of the reported sightings could be attributed to natural phenomena, misidentifications of aircraft, weather balloons, astronomical objects, and other explainable events. The program concluded that there was no evidence to suggest that UFOs were of extraterrestrial origin or that they posed any threat to national security.

In 1969, the Condon Committee, a scientific review board at the University of Colorado, conducted an assessment of Project Blue Book's methodology and findings. The Condon Committee, officially known as the "University of Colorado UFO Project," was a scientific study board commissioned by the United States Air Force to assess the validity of UFO reports and to evaluate whether further investigation into UFOs was warranted. The committee was named after its director, Dr. Edward U. Condon, a prominent physicist.

The committee's final report, commonly referred to as the "Condon Report," was published in 1969. The report concluded that the majority of UFO sightings could be explained by conventional and natural phenomena and that there was no evidence to suggest that UFOs represented a threat to national security or that they were of extraterrestrial origin. The committee also concluded that further study of UFOs was unlikely to yield significant scientific discoveries.

The Condon Report effectively marked the decline of official U.S. government interest and funding in UFO research. After its publication, Project Blue Book was officially shut down, and the Air Force ceased its active investigations into UFO reports.

1995: Robert Bigelow's NIDS

Nevertheless, the Condon report did not mark the end of the intrigue surrounding UFOs. Over the subsequent decades, self-proclaimed "UFOlogists" continued to submit freedom of information requests to federal agencies in their pursuit of unearthing information about these sightings.

In 1995, entrepreneur Robert Bigelow assembled a small team of experts in Las Vegas to explore the potential existence of extraterrestrial life. This group was named the National Institute for Discovery Science (NIDS). It included notable participants such as former astronauts Ed Mitchell and Harrison Schmitt, alongside sitting U.S. Senator Harry Reid, a Democrat representing Nevada.

NIDS had a dedicated focus on investigating a spectrum of scientific enigmas and unexplained occurrences, among them UFOs. What set NIDS apart was its analytical and scientific approach toward scrutinizing the array of mystifying data. These encompassed not only UFO sightings but also instances of cattle mutilations and other paranormal happenings.

NIDS adopted a distinctive strategy of meticulously collecting data, conducting thorough on-site examinations, and fostering collaboration with experts from diverse domains like aerospace, physics, and psychology.

In 2004, NIDS ceased its operations suddenly, but the exact rationale behind this decision remains unknown. Following NIDS's closure, its founder, Robert Bigelow, created Bigelow Aerospace, a company dedicated to pioneering space technology and habitats.

2004: An Encounter At Sea off San Diego

In November 2004, during a flight training mission, two Navy pilots were instructed to intercept an unknown aircraft. They visually identified and followed an unconventional oval-shaped craft, approximately 40 feet in length, hovering above the Pacific Ocean, roughly a hundred miles off the coast of San Diego. Before the pilots could close in, the craft accelerated away at a high speed.

It all started when the pilots took off in an F/A-18 Super Hornet from the flight deck of the U.S.S. Nimitz aircraft carrier. Shortly after takeoff, they spotted an elongated object just hovering above the water's surface.

Suddenly, the object speeded up, rising to between 500 to 1,000 feet while maintaining a speed of around 500 knots. Remarkably, the jet aircraft's onboard radar failed to detect the object. However, the aircraft Weapons Systems Operator (WSO) seated in the rear saw and corroborated the sighting.

Both the aviators communicated with each other so that both of them confirmed that they saw the object visually. Then, the craft moved suddenly at a very high speed that the pilots had to struggle to keep pace with it.

Given their expertise in identifying aircraft based on visual cues such as shapes, paint schemes, and unit emblems, military pilots possess a good ability to distinguish between various aircraft. However, the pilots said this craft was beyond any recognizable aircraft or flying object within their knowledge.

Two additional Super Hornets were deployed and were airborne, forewarned about the anomaly. One of these jets managed to capture the object's image using a forward-looking infrared camera. The alien craft, with a length of 40 feet, possessed a smooth, round exterior and was promptly given the moniker "Tic-Tac."

Despite infrared validation, when the pilots reported their encounter, it garnered minimal attention from their superiors, and subsequently, their fellow aviators subjected them to jokes and puns about extraterrestrials, and the matter, though reported, was soon forgotten.

2007: A New Pentagon Investigation

With support from the majority leader of the U.S. Senate, the Pentagon initiated the Advanced Aerospace Threat Identification Program (AATIP) to evaluate the recent series of sightings.

The agency stated in briefing documents, "What was once confined to science fiction has now turned into a scientific reality." The program was managed by a military intelligence officer and collaborated with a private aerospace research company.

AATIP, an undisclosed U.S. government endeavor, concentrated on investigating unidentified aerial phenomena (UAPs), commonly known as UFOs. Its existence became public in 2017 through media reports and official statements.

Initially funded through the Defense Intelligence Agency's (DIA) budget, AATIP was established to probe reports of UAPs displaying advanced aviation and aerospace capabilities beyond known human-made aircraft. It became widely known that the program had received around $22 million in funding from 2007 to 2012.

The program's core efforts regarding UFOs encompassed gathering and scrutinizing data from diverse sources, such as military personnel, radar systems, and eyewitness testimonials of UAP sightings. The intention was to discern patterns, behaviors, and traits of these UAPs, evaluating whether they posed any potential security threats.

Advanced Technology Assessment: AATIP's focus included identifying any technological advancements linked to observed UAPs. This involved analyzing flight capacities, propulsion systems, and other attributes of these phenomena. The objective was to determine if foreign adversaries possessed advanced aerospace technologies observed in the UAP encounters.

In 2017, film footage recorded by military pilots showing interactions with UAPs was publicly disclosed, resulting in significant interest and discussions. These included the so-called "Tic-Tac" and "Gimbal" clips, capturing UAP flight behaviors that showcased their challenging and conventional aerodynamic-defying capabilities.

AATIP's revelation and its findings increased public curiosity about UFOs and UAPs. Despite its formal conclusion in 2012, the Pentagon confirmed sustained interest in the UAP matter, explored through alternate means. In 2020, the Pentagon formally established the Unidentified Aerial Phenomena (UAP) Task Force to go deeper into these sightings.

These revelations and discussions have prompted calls for heightened government transparency in reporting and probing such phenomena. While many of these sightings remain unexplained, the acknowledgment of AATIP by the U.S. government renewed attention to UFOs and their potential implications.

2014: Increased Sightings and Encounters

During this period, Navy pilots documented and filmed a series of interactions with unidentified craft capable of attaining high altitudes and hypersonic speeds.

Interest in these sightings varied but peaked notably in late 2014 and early 2015. Super Hornets positioned on the U.S.S. Roosevelt began encountering fast-moving, unidentifiable aircraft resembling, as described by a pilot, "a cube inside a sphere." These upgraded radar-equipped aircraft successfully tracked the peculiar targets. In the subsequent year, three gun-camera videos recorded flying objects, now known as "Gimbal" and "Go-Fast."

Though the naval aviators who recorded the footage remain unnamed, two pilots have emerged as witnesses. In both 2014 and 2015, they observed anomalous signals on their radar screens and captured wingless, tailless objects on their aircraft's video cameras. These pilots and others, who have not been identified, spotted objects at varying altitudes, including sea level, and with acceleration to hypersonic speeds exceeding five times the speed of sound. Some demonstrated remarkable endurance, staying airborne for up to 12 hours without any apparent need for refueling. A few appeared to submerge into the sea, as recorded and filmed by Navy aviators.

2017: Public Revelation

These events and investigations remained largely undisclosed to the general public until December 2017, when the New York Times disclosed to the public the Pentagon's Advanced Aerospace Threat Identification Program (AATIP). Despite Pentagon officials asserting the program's conclusion in 2012, this revelation spurred fresh interest in UFOs among the public, media, and even the scientific community.

2020: A Call to Action

In July 2020, an article published in Scientific American magazine written by NASA scientists suggested a re-evaluation of the Condon report's conclusions. They acknowledged that while some Unidentified Aerial Phenomena (UAP) events might be attributed to classified military aircraft, weather anomalies, or misidentifications, there remained genuinely perplexing cases warranting further inquiry.

Responding to ongoing mysteries in the skies, the Pentagon established the Unidentified Aerial Phenomena Task Force (UAPTF) in August 2020. The task force aimed to enhance comprehension and insights into the origin and nature of these unexplained objects.

2021: Unidentified Aerial Phenomena Report

Moving into 2021, an unclassified report released by the Office of The Director of National Intelligence dated June 25 addressed the issue. The report revealed that the vast majority of over 120 sightings spanning two decades could not be ascribed to any known US military or government technology.

This conclusion effectively ruled out the possibility that military pilots encountering these phenomena had stumbled upon secret US government initiatives. However, the report's conclusiveness largely ended there, leaving room for the potential that these occurrences might involve unidentified craft, possibly of extraterrestrial origin.

The report acknowledged the challenge of explaining the peculiar flight behaviors of the crafts, such as sudden acceleration and changes in direction at varying speeds during these encounters. The possibility of these being weather balloons or similar objects was considered but rejected.

Most reported UAP instances likely involved tangible objects observed by multiple sensors such as radar, infrared, electro-optical devices, weapon seekers, and visual observations. Nevertheless, a few incidents showcased unusual flight characteristics, potentially stemming from sensor errors, spoofing, or observer misinterpretations, necessitating thorough analysis. The report noted that the sensors on military platforms were not primarily designed for UAP identification.

The report also explored incidents involving unidentified crafts of foreign military forces, speculating that certain sightings could be experimental technologies from rival states, with China or Russia being likely contenders.

The report ultimately admitted that the limited quantity of reliable UAP reports hindered drawing concrete conclusions regarding their nature or intent. However, it acknowledged the ongoing active evaluation of UFOs through the Department of Defense Unidentified Aerial Phenomena Task Force (UAPTF).

2022: NASA Jumps In To Investigate

In April 2022, the Pentagon made a significant move by introducing the All-domain Anomaly Resolution Office, an entity established with the purpose of investigating objects that could potentially pose a threat to national security.

In the following June, NASA took a parallel yet distinct initiative. The space agency revealed plans to institute an independent study program dedicated to comprehensively addressing the matter from a scientific perspective. In their announcement, they outlined their intention to identify existing data from a wide spectrum of sources, including civilians, government agencies, nonprofits, and companies. Additionally, they aimed to determine further data collection requirements and formulate effective analytical methodologies.

Adding another layer to the evolving narrative, the year 2022 marked an alteration in nomenclature. The term "Unidentified Aerial Phenomena" underwent an official transformation, as it is now called "Unidentified Anomalous Phenomena."

2023: The Truth is Still Out There

Moving into 2023, the veil of mystery surrounding these phenomena still remains largely intact. The Director of National Intelligence (DNI) presented an updated report in June 2023, disclosing an additional 510 sightings. Out of these, 171 instances remained perplexing. In these cases, unidentified craft often exhibited unconventional flight behaviors and performance capabilities, which raised intrigue and warranted scrutiny.

Notably, former intelligence official and whistleblower David Grusch emerged in the spotlight, bringing the UFO controversy to the forefront. Despite the Pentagon's vigorous denial of his claims, Grusch steadfastly adhered to his testimony, intensifying the public discourse around the issue.

While the scientific community has been actively seeking signs of extraterrestrial life for years, definitive results have remained elusive thus far. NASA designates this pursuit as one of its key goals. Given the astronomical number of planets and moons within the universe, counted in billions and trillions, the notion that Earth is the only planet with intelligent life seems improbable. However, whether conclusive evidence will emerge in the near future is an open question that remains elusive, shrouded in anticipation and uncertainty.

Chapter 5

UFOlogy and Popular Culture

"E.T. THE EXTRA-TERRESTRIAL" IS a science fiction film directed by Steven Spielberg and released in 1982. The movie follows the story of an extra-terrestrial being who is accidentally left behind by his spaceship while visiting Earth. Elliot, a young boy discovers the alien in his garage, names him E.T., and befriends him.

E.T. struggles to find ways to communicate with his spaceship with no communication device of his own. He tries to make a rudimentary device using parts of a kids' electronic game and other household items without much success.

Elliot discovers that E.T.'s health is deteriorating rapidly and becomes increasingly weak. He realizes that the only way to help E.T. is to use his connection with the alien to save him. With the help of his friends, he brings E.T. to his backyard, where they set up the communication device he built. Elliot connects himself to E.T. by holding his hand, and through their emotional bond, they manage to power up the device.

In a moment of sheer magic, E.T. uses the device to initiate a telekinetic link between himself, Elliot, and the bicycle of Elliot. With John Williams' dramatic music score in the background, the bicycle begins to lift off the ground, defying gravity. The scene captures the sense of exhilaration and awe as the kid soars into the night sky, silhouetted against the full moon. Although scared, the boy feels a sense of liberation from the constraints of Earth, which creates a beautiful, heartwarming moment.

The bicycle flying scene is not only a visual spectacle but also shows that a bond of friendship between humans and aliens is possible. It's a moment that showcases the power of love, the wonder of discovery, and the triumph of innocence over fear. This scene has become a symbol of the film's theme and remains a memorable moment in cinematic history.

Soon, the spaceship receives the emergency signal and returns to rescue E.T. Elliot and his friends have to say an emotional goodbye to E.T. as he returns to his spaceship and flies back to his world.

Hollywood's Fascination with UFOs and Extra-terrestrials

Hollywood has always been captivated by the mysteries of UFOs and aliens, producing a variety of films that show the glamor and mystery and have portrayed both benevolent and adversarial encounters with aliens from beyond our world.

For decades, the mass appeal of UFOs and the mysterious fascination with extraterrestrial beings have played out on the silver screen. A combination of cultural, psychological, and creative themes harmoniously show their charm in this captivating interaction between humans and creatures from other worlds.

The deep curiosity within us reaches its peak when we think about the mysteries of the universe. The idea of life beyond Earth and advanced civilizations we can't reach excites us, inviting us to explore the unknown. UFOs and aliens have a captivating charm, blending the mysterious with the irresistible in storytelling. Filmmakers capture this fantasy while showing the excitement and skill of their craft.

But these stories aren't just intriguing; they mirror our beliefs and fears. The silver screen reflects our struggles with identity, our fears of what we don't know, and the results of our choices.

Filmmakers use extraterrestrial characters to bring out diversity, courage, strength, and personal growth. These beings from other galaxies embody our own conflicts, encouraging us to look inside and grow.

These tales aren't just fiction; they let us escape reality. They tempt us to go beyond what's familiar and explore the extraordinary. In this world, the impossible becomes possible, and our imaginations wander free from any constraints.

Thanks to computer-generated graphics, filmmakers create amazing creatures and alien landscapes that stick in our minds. These visual wonders use technology to make these stories unforgettable.

In the end, what makes UFOs and aliens appealing to Hollywood is their power to captivate us. This fascination shows our desire to understand our existence, find others like us, and discover stories that light up our imagination.

And, of course, it's all for fun. Plus, it's good for Hollywood's business – making money from movies is their bread and butter, after all; countless movies have UFOs and aliens as their main themes, and here is a roundup of a few of them:

"Close Encounters of the Third Kind" (1977)

Directed by Steven Spielberg, this iconic film presents a narrative where aliens are shown as friendly beings without any harmful intentions toward humans. The movie suggests that we can communicate with aliens from advanced civilizations. The story revolves around encounters between humans and aliens, emphasizing the idea of peaceful interaction and mutual understanding.

"Independence Day" (1996)

Directed by Roland Emmerich, this film features a massive alien invasion that seriously threatens humanity's survival. The movie showcases the colossal destruction caused by the invading aliens and portrays humanity's united efforts to resist the intruders. The story follows a group of people who come together to fight against the aliens and defend Earth.

"Men in Black" (1997)

Barry Sonnenfeld's sci-fi comedy offers a humorous take on aliens and government secrecy. The film introduces a covert government agency responsible for overseeing and regulating alien activity on Earth. It combines humor with conspiracy-laden intrigue, following the adventures of agents who work to keep alien-related incidents under control.

"Signs" (2002)

Directed by M. Night Shyamalan, "Signs" weaves a tale centered on a family's experiences with crop circles and mysterious events occurring on their farm. The film explores themes of faith, fear, and the unexplained, maintaining a suspenseful atmosphere throughout. It probes into how the family grapples with the unknown and their reactions to inexplicable phenomena.

"War of the Worlds" (2005)

Steven Spielberg's adaptation of H.G. Wells' novel portrays a cataclysmic alien attack on Earth. The film focuses on a family's struggle for survival as they face the chaos and destruction caused by the technologically advanced alien invaders. It explores human vulnerability and the challenges humans face when confronted with an overwhelmingly superior force.

"District 9" (2009)

Directed by Neill Blomkamp, this thought-provoking narrative is set in a world where alien refugees are confined to a slum in Johannesburg. The film explores themes of discrimination, segregation, and the consequences of initial contact between humans and aliens. It highlights the complexities of societal reactions to the arrival of extraterrestrial beings.

"Arrival" (2016)

Directed by Denis Villeneuve, "Arrival" takes an intellectual approach to alien encounters. The film follows a linguist's efforts to communicate with mysterious aliens who have arrived on Earth. It investigates themes of language, time, and mutual comprehension, offering a unique exploration of how humans and aliens might interact.

"The Arrival" (1996)

Starring Charlie Sheen, this film centers on a radio astronomer who discovers evidence of an alien signal. As he investigates further, he becomes entangled in a web of conspiracy related to an impending alien invasion. The movie explores the suspenseful journey of unraveling the truth behind the alien signal and its implications for humanity.

These films encompass a broad spectrum of perspectives on UFOs and aliens, ranging from heartwarming stories of companionship to nerve-racking encounters and profound meditations on humanity's response to the unknown. The magic of these themes continues to enthrall audiences and fuel the creative fire of filmmakers.

The X-Files Phenomenon: How Fiction Influences Belief

"The X-Files" is a TV show that explores mysterious things like UFOs and government secrets. One big idea in "The X-Files" is how real and made-up things mix seamlessly. The show talks about things like aliens and weird events, which makes people think about what's real and what's not.

The characters Mulder and Scully made us think about strange stuff in a new way. People started to wonder about aliens and what was out in space, just like the characters did. Mulder's unyielding pursuit of truth and Scully's skeptical yet open-minded approach mirrors the tension between skepticism and curiosity that exists in our minds.

The show also made people actually believe in things like aliens and government secrets. People who saw UFOs or thought about secret plans felt like the show understood them.

The show's impact transcended entertainment, giving rise to a subculture of believers who, influenced by the series' themes, started their own quest for the truth.

Did the show just talk about things people already believed, or did it make them believe new things? It made people think differently and that what we imagine can change what we think is true, just like facts can.

The connection between stories and what we think is a two-way street. "The X-Files" did this by telling stories that made us want to know more about strange things. It made us want to understand things that are hard to explain.

"The X-Files" is still a very popular TV series, and it is a good example of how movies can change our perception even about things that are very strange and implausible.

UFOs in Art, Music, and Literature

The idea of UFOs, those mysterious flying objects, has become a really interesting part of human culture. It's not just in one area – it's in art, music, and literature too. This fascination with UFOs has spread widely and has had a big impact on our culture. It shows that things we don't understand can make us think in creative ways and make us stop and think.

Art

Throughout history, artists have liked the idea of aliens and flying objects we can't identify. They've shown this in cave drawings, paintings from a long time ago, and even in modern art. These UFOs usually mean something mysterious and amazing. The thought of creatures from other places makes artists think about big things, like stuff that's really great and exciting, and things beyond where we live.

Certain well-known artworks actually contain hidden elements related to UFOs. These elements blend the sense of something extraordinary with the ordinary world around them. It's like a combination of magic and the everyday that artists have cleverly woven into their creations.

Picture people sitting around a fire in a cave, their shadows dancing on the walls. Even back then, they were drawing stars and planets. Move forward to a time called the Renaissance, when artists used canvas and paint to explore new ideas. They imagined extraterrestrial beings and their touch, shown as flying things, in the amazing paintings of artists like da Vinci and Raphael. These artworks are kind of mysterious and make us want to look beyond what we know and see something bigger.

This fascination with UFOs didn't go away; it kept going and came to modern art. Here, the idea of UFOs gets mixed with new kinds of art to make something interesting. Through bright colors, brushstrokes, and modern tools, artists make us think about space and the unknown. In

Salvador Dalí's painting "The Sacrament of the Last Supper," something like a spaceship is there, making us feel like we're connecting with something beyond us. In Hieronymus Bosch's "The Garden of Earthly Delights," a strange flying thing goes through unusual places, watching the world and the sky.

But these UFOs aren't just cool things to look at. They also show how we all want to go beyond what we know, explore things we don't understand, and look at the amazing parts of the universe. The idea of UFOs in art is like a dance between what's real and what's imagined, a beautiful mix of things we know and things we're still learning about.

Music

UFOs have inspired a lot of music, making a big impact on how it sounds. This influence has created different kinds of music, from peaceful and spacey to really exciting and strange. Musicians from all sorts of music styles have been interested in UFO stories, and they've added this feeling to their music, giving listeners a spacey experience.

Imagine music notes floating through space, capturing the feeling of things we don't understand. Artists love this kind of music because it matches the mysterious stories we hear about stars. For example, songs like David Bowie's "Starman" and Pink Floyd's "Set the Controls for the Heart of the Sun" create a musical journey that feels like we are in outer space. These musicians make us feel like we're part of something big beyond what we usually know.

But UFO-inspired music isn't only in rock and roll. Electronic music, like the kind Jean-Michel Jarre makes, is another way to feel this experience. His electronic music takes us on a trip through space like we're on a sound spaceship. The layers of sound, rhythm, and melody make us feel like we're in space, thinking about UFOs and their mysteries.

In this music, we can hear the feelings and thoughts that UFOs bring out in us. The spooky sounds, the beats, and the spacey melodies guide us through the emotions that thinking about space and UFOs can bring. This music isn't just sounds; it's like an invitation to explore the mysterious and get lost in the music that makes us think about things we don't know.

In the soft notes and the loud parts that go on for a while, we can see how UFOs have changed music. This music helps us feel like we're going to space, connecting what's on Earth to the mysteries of the universe. When we listen, we become like space travelers, going on a journey not just through musical notes but through the feelings of the universe's mysteries. UFOs have left their mark on music, making melodies and rhythms that make us think about the unknown in a way everyone can understand.

Literature

Throughout history, writers have used words to explore the mystery of UFOs and the idea of life beyond Earth. From old-fashioned pens to modern keyboards, books have shown our endless interest in what's out there in space. These stories let us travel through space in our minds, connecting things from Earth to the universe.

Think about famous writers and how they've used their imagination like spaceships to understand things we don't know. In H.G. Wells' book "The War of the Worlds," words made a story about aliens coming to Victorian England. It wasn't just a made-up tale; it made us think about what it would be like if aliens actually visited us.

In Arthur C. Clarke's "Childhood's End," words helped us see beyond what we know. The story took us on a journey that felt like going to space, where we learned about things we couldn't fully understand. The characters in the story felt the same way we might feel if we met aliens.

But UFOs in stories mean more than just exciting plots. They're like mirrors showing how people think and feel in society. Writers use the idea of aliens to talk about our worries, dreams, and hopes. These stories show how we're scared, want to be saved, and sometimes feel confused.

Aliens in stories can be signs of big changes or new beginnings. They might save us from bad things, or they could make things crazy and uncertain. These stories are like keys that unlock ideas about what could happen in the future.

By putting UFOs and extra-terrestrials in their stories, writers invite us to think about things that are far away and hard to understand. As we read, we explore space and time in our minds.

The way fiction mixes with reality makes us think about what's out there and how we fit into the universe. Just like space explorers, we journey through these stories and imagine what could be beyond our world.

UFOs and Aliens in Comic Books

UFOs and aliens have been popular themes in comic books for a long time. These stories often take readers on exciting adventures that involve encounters with extraterrestrial beings and their advanced technology.

UFOs are depicted as mysterious flying objects from outer space. They can come in various shapes and sizes, adding an element of suspense and wonder to the stories and illustrations.

Sometimes, these UFOs are piloted by aliens who are either friendly or hostile, leading to thrilling conflicts and alliances with the human characters.

Aliens in comic books also come in diverse forms. Some are depicted as humanoid beings with unique powers and abilities, while others might be completely different from anything we've seen on Earth. These alien characters often bring their own cultures, societies, and conflicts into the stories, adding depth and complexity to the comic book universes.

Comic books provide a platform for exploring different aspects of UFOs and alien encounters. Some stories focus on the excitement of first contact, while others delve into the challenges of understanding and communicating with beings from other planets. Themes of exploration, curiosity, and the unknown are commonly woven into these narratives.

Comic books offer a creative space where writers and artists can imagine imaginative scenarios involving UFOs and aliens, captivating readers with tales of adventure, discovery, and the mysteries of the cosmos.

The Grand Design

In the big picture of human culture, UFOs are more than just symbols. They're like guiding lights that help us explore new ideas and think about things. This influence from UFOs is like a beautiful artwork made up of many small pieces.

They make us curious, spark our imagination, and make us think. It is seen everywhere, going beyond limits and styles. It makes us ask big questions about space, what we know, and things we don't. In art, music, and stories,

We want to understand the big and unknown parts of the universe. This influence from UFOs stays with us because it's so interesting. It reminds us that we're always excited about space and the unknown. This excitement shows up in what we create and how we see ourselves as a culture.

Chapter 6

A Litany of Hoaxes and Conspiracies

A RADIO SHOW BASED on the H.G Wells novel "War of the Worlds" was created by Orson Welles and was aired on October 30, 1938. The show presented the story as a series of dramatic news bulletins reporting a Martian invasion of Earth. Some listeners believed it to be true that an actual Martian invasion was taking place. It caused widespread unrest among the general public.

The show began with a regular programming announcement, followed by a music performance, which then transitioned into a weather report. Soon after, the show started to interrupt the music and reports with urgent news updates about an alien craft landing in New Jersey.

The fictional news bulletins became increasingly alarming, reporting strange occurrences and detailing a Martian invasion. Listeners who tuned in after the introduction may not have realized it was a dramatization, as they missed the disclaimer at the start of the show. The realistic and intense delivery of the news updates led many people to believe that a genuine extraterrestrial invasion was happening.

Panic and confusion spread as the broadcast continued, with some listeners reportedly fleeing their homes and others calling authorities for confirmation. It wasn't until later in the broadcast that the show's true nature was revealed.

Although it was an unintended hoax, Orson Welles' adaptation demonstrated the power of media and storytelling to influence public perception and generate strong emotional responses.

This historical event serves as a reminder of the impact that communication and media can have on society, highlighting the importance of responsible and accurate reporting in shaping public understanding.

The role of media regarding UFOs and aliens is complex and multi-faceted. Media plays a significant role in shaping public perception, disseminating information, and influencing cultural attitudes towards these topics.

Media serves as a platform for sharing information about UFO sightings, alleged encounters with extraterrestrial beings, and related phenomena. UFOs and aliens often generate discussions among the general public, experts, and enthusiasts when reported by the media.

Media is a double-edged sword when it comes to UFOs and aliens. While it has the power to educate, inspire, and engage, it also has the potential to spread misinformation and sensationalism.

Hoaxes

There have been several famous hoaxes related to UFOs and aliens throughout history. These hoaxes often capture public attention and spark debates about the credibility of UFO sightings and extraterrestrial claims.

The Alien Autopsy Film (1995)

The Roswell UFO Incident of 1947 was not itself a hoax, but the U.S. military was embroiled in it, initially stating that the debris of alien craft had been recovered then but later reverted their claim and called it a weather balloon.

Conspiracy theories claim that the military covered up the crash of an alien spacecraft, but investigations have found no substantial evidence to support these claims.

But what was really a big hoax was a film that surfaced in 1995 claiming it to depict an autopsy performed on an extraterrestrial being that was recovered from the Roswell crash. The footage showed surgeons dissecting a humanoid creature. However, the film was later exposed as a hoax created by special effects artists, and the "alien" was revealed to be a prop.

Gulf Breeze UFO Photos (1987)

A series of UFO photographs taken in Gulf Breeze, Florida, gained attention in the late 1980s. The photographer claimed to have captured images of UFOs drifting in the sky. Even many experts thought that the photographs were genuine.

In 1990, after the photographer and his family had moved from their home, the new owners of their house discovered a styrofoam model UFO hidden in the attic. The journalist covering the story later used the models to duplicate almost exactly the original photographs, proving that the original images were fake photographs.

Billy Meier's UFO Photos (1970s-1980s)

Billy Meier was a Swiss national who gained attention when he claimed that he had been in contact with extraterrestrial beings from the Pleiades star cluster, the Plejaren. He also claimed that these beings shared spiritual and philosophical teachings with him.

His claims caused great interest among some UFO enthusiasts, as he insisted that he had a collection of photographs and videos of UFOs and Plejaren spacecraft. The photographs showed disc-shaped craft, often flying over Swiss landscapes. However, skeptics questioned his credentials and declared him a fake. The photos were later revealed to be made using props, models, and double exposure techniques.

These examples highlight the diverse ways in which hoaxes related to UFOs and aliens have captured the public's imagination over the years. They serve as a reminder to critically evaluate and scrutinize extraordinary claims, especially in the absence of credible evidence.

Conspiracy Theories

There are several popular conspiracy theories regarding UFOs and extraterrestrial life. These theories are not supported by mainstream science and lack substantial evidence, but are still popular in UFOlogy.

Area 51

Area 51 is a highly classified U.S. Air Force facility located in the Nevada desert. For years, it has been a focal point of conspiracy theories, primarily due to its secrecy and the nature of its operations.

Conspiracy theories surrounding Area 51 often tie back to UFOs and extraterrestrial life. Some believe that the facility is a hub for reverse-engineering alien technology recovered from crashed UFOs.

These theories are fueled by reports of strange aircraft sightings near Area 51, as well as accounts from alleged former employees and whistleblowers who claim to have seen advanced extraterrestrial technology within the facility.

Additionally, some theories propose that Area 51 serves as a base for government interactions with extraterrestrial beings, with rumors of secret underground facilities and covert experiments adding to the mystique.

Some theories suggest that wreckage from the Roswell crash was transported to Area 51 for analysis and reverse engineering. This narrative has contributed to the aura of secrecy and intrigue surrounding both events.

While these conspiracy theories are compelling and have captured the public's imagination, there is limited concrete evidence to support them. The U.S. government's changing explanations for the Roswell incident have certainly fueled suspicions, but alternative explanations, such as classified military projects, can be the probable reason for its secrecy.

Majestic 12 (MJ-12)

The MJ-12 conspiracy is a fascinating and debated theory that revolves around the alleged existence of a secret government committee formed in the 1940s to manage and conceal information related to extraterrestrial contact and UFO sightings.

The origin of the MJ-12 conspiracy dates back to the late 1980s when a set of documents, known as the "Majestic 12 documents," surfaced. These documents purportedly provided evidence of the existence of a top-secret group formed by an executive order by President Harry S. Truman in 1947.

The committee, consisting of influential scientists, military personnel, and government officials, was allegedly tasked with overseeing the recovery and investigation of crashed UFOs and interactions with extraterrestrial beings.

While the concept of a shadowy government agency managing such affairs might sound like a plot from a science fiction movie, the authenticity of the MJ-12 documents has been a subject of heated debate. Skeptics argue that the documents are likely hoaxes or fabrications.

Alien Malfeasances

The concept of alien abductions revolves around the belief that individuals are taken against their will by extraterrestrial beings for various purposes, often involving medical examinations and experiments. These accounts typically describe experiences of being transported aboard spacecraft and subjected to strange procedures.

Conspiracy theories surrounding alien abductions touch on themes of government cover-ups, psychological manipulation, and advanced technology.

Some theorists suggest that these abductions might be part of a larger agenda involving secret collaborations between governments and alien species. However, these accounts are largely anecdotal and lack concrete evidence.

Mutilations of cattle are a shock to local farmers that seem to defy natural explanations. Theories surrounding cattle mutilations often connect them to extraterrestrial activities, suggesting that the precision of the mutilations and the absence of visible signs of struggle imply the involvement of advanced technology.

These mutilations are explained as part of a larger phenomenon involving scientific research conducted by alien entities. Some theories even speculate that cattle mutilations are attempts to study the effects of environmental pollution and its impact on living organisms. Skeptics, on the other hand, attribute the mutilations to natural causes, such as scavenging animals or decomposition.

Black helicopters

The black helicopters conspiracy theory centers around the belief that unmarked black helicopters that are seen around UFO sightings are part of covert government operations or surveillance. These helicopters may be associated with secret military projects, government surveillance, and even alien encounters.

It is suggested that these helicopters are used by shadowy government organizations to monitor and control civilian populations, conduct clandestine missions, or facilitate the cover-up of extraterrestrial activities. While some sightings of black helicopters have been attributed to legitimate military and law enforcement operations, the idea of sinister motives behind them is enough to captivate conspiracy enthusiasts.

Some UFO enthusiasts believe these helicopters are used to cover up UFO encounters or transport recovered UFO debris and alien bodies. These ideas are part of broader conspiracy narratives involving secret government agencies and extraterrestrial contact.

Secret Technologies

An intriguing theory that proposes UFO sightings may not necessarily be evidence of extraterrestrial visitors but rather the result of advanced secret technologies developed by governments or military organizations.

Many UFO sightings describe objects exhibiting sudden changes in speed, direction, and even apparent anti-gravity effects. This has led some theorists to suggest that governments have achieved breakthroughs in propulsion systems, potentially involving exotic concepts like anti-gravity, electromagnetic manipulation, or other advanced energy sources.

One key aspect of this theory is the concept of reverse engineering. According to this line of thought, governments may have recovered and studied unidentified alien objects, potentially even crash debris, and used their findings to develop cutting-edge technologies. This process involves dissecting and analyzing the recovered material to understand its mechanics and then attempting to recreate or adapt those principles for human applications.

Black projects, which are highly classified and often undisclosed research and development initiatives, are often cited in this context. These projects are known to involve top scientists, engineers, and experts working on revolutionary technologies outside the public domain. Advocates of the theory propose that these black projects could be responsible for some of the observed UFO phenomena.

Reptilian Overlords

The Reptilian Overlords is a very bizarre conspiracy theory that suggests that a secretive group of shape-shifting reptilian beings, hailing from another planet or even another dimension, has surreptitiously infiltrated our human society. Their ultimate goal is to assert control and manipulate humanity to further their mysterious agendas.

This outlandish concept envisions these reptilian entities as having the uncanny ability to morph into human form, allowing them to seamlessly blend into our everyday lives while secretly wielding their influence.

The origins of the Reptilian Overlords theory have threads that extend far back in history, drawing inspiration from ancient myths and cultural stories that featured reptilian deities and beings. However, it found new life in the modern era, fueled by a mix of science fiction, conspiracy literature, and the burgeoning interest in UFOs and the paranormal.

According to proponents, they have cunningly integrated themselves into positions of power, whether in politics, celebrity circles, or other influential spheres. In this hidden capacity, they're believed to covertly manipulate global events, financial systems, and even the decisions of world leaders, all while following their cryptic agendas.

Some versions propose that certain powerful families are direct descendants of these enigmatic reptilian beings. This concept intricately weaves together notions of hereditary lines and obscured hierarchies that secretly govern the world.

Conspiracy theorists also often point to symbolism as evidence of the reptilian influence. They scrutinize ancient and contemporary art, architecture, and even pop culture for hidden meanings and messages. Symbols like snakes and reptilian motifs are interpreted as veiled signals of their presence.

However, experts, scientists, and skeptics widely dismiss the Reptilian Overlords theory. They emphasize the glaring lack of tangible evidence supporting the existence of these shape-shifting reptilian beings. Moreover, the claims made by the theory's proponents often defy logic and rational scrutiny.

Alien Bases on the Moon

This suggests that the lunar surface might harbor hidden installations or structures built by extraterrestrial civilizations. Some proponents of this theory claim that these bases are either active or remnants of past alien presence, serving as monitoring stations or research facilities.

Those who support the idea of Alien Bases on the Moon often analyze lunar images and anomalies in satellite photos to point out unusual formations that could be interpreted as artificial structures. They argue that governments and space agencies might be involved in a cover-up to conceal the existence of these extraterrestrial bases.

However, the scientific community generally dismisses this theory due to a lack of credible evidence. Lunar exploration missions, including the Apollo missions and more recent satellite missions, have provided extensive data and images that are consistent with natural geological processes. What may seem like unusual formations at first glance can often be explained by impact cratering, volcanic activity, or other known lunar processes.

Project Blue Beam and Fake Alien Invasion

Project Blue Beam is a strange conspiracy theory that suggests a covert plan by the government or powerful entities to deceive the public through advanced technology, including holographic projections and mind control. According to this theory, the goal of Project Blue Beam is to manipulate human beliefs and perceptions on a global scale, potentially leading to the establishment of a New World Order.

The concept of a Fake Alien Invasion is closely related to Project Blue Beam. It revolves around the idea that a staged alien invasion will be used to achieve geopolitical goals or maintain social control.

Proponents of this theory suggest that powerful entities might create a false extraterrestrial threat to manipulate public opinion and justify increased military spending, technological development, and the erosion of civil liberties.

The Fake Alien Invasion could take various forms, including holographic projections, false news reports, or even the use of advanced aircraft designed to resemble alien spacecraft. The goal would be to create panic and chaos, thereby uniting humanity under a global authority that claims to protect against the alien threat.

Both Project Blue Beam and the Fake Alien Invasion theory are highly controversial and speculative. Skeptics point out that the technical challenges of creating convincing holographic projections on a global scale are immense, and the implementation of mass mind control is ethically and scientifically questionable. Additionally, the idea that governments or powerful entities could orchestrate such elaborate deceptions without detection raises questions about the plausibility of these theories.

Secret Agreements with Aliens

The notion of secret agreements with aliens is a captivating and speculative concept often explored in the realm of UFO and extraterrestrial theories. This theory suggests that governments or shadowy organizations have entered into covert pacts or negotiations with advanced extraterrestrial beings. These alleged agreements could encompass various aspects, ranging from technology exchange to collaboration on global affairs.

Proponents of this theory propose that advanced alien civilizations possess knowledge and technology far beyond our own. Secret agreements are believed to involve the exchange of alien technology for various concessions or resources, allowing governments to harness these advancements for military, scientific, or economic purposes.

Some versions of this theory posit that extraterrestrial beings might share common interests with governments, such as environmental protection or the prevention of large-scale conflicts. The idea is that these advanced civilizations might be willing to offer assistance in exchange for cooperation on specific objectives.

Supporters of the theory argue that these agreements are kept hidden from the public due to concerns about potential panic, disruption of societal norms, or the preservation of geopolitical power structures. Secrecy is maintained to ensure strict confidentiality and compartmentalization to prevent leaks.

The concept of secret agreements with aliens without any solid evidence, coupled with the fantastical nature of the claims, makes it difficult to substantiate these theories.

Extraterrestrial Gods and Religions

This theory suggests that advanced alien civilizations might have instigated or even directly shaped our spiritual beliefs, traditions, and religious practices.

At its heart, this theory paints a picture of ancient civilizations being visited by beings from beyond our planet—entities possessing advanced knowledge, technology, and an understanding of human psychology that appeared godlike in their capabilities. These extraterrestrial visitors, often portrayed as gods or divine messengers, are purported to have played a significant role in shaping the tapestry of human spirituality.

This theory proposes that advanced extraterrestrial beings were mistaken for gods by ancient civilizations. Proponents suggest that religious texts and ancient monuments contain evidence of contact with these beings, implying that human religions were influenced by interactions with alien visitors.

Stories of gods descending from the heavens, offering profound wisdom, and guiding humanity's path are reconsidered as potential accounts of these cosmic encounters. The introduction of advanced religious concepts by these extraterrestrial beings could have catalyzed the development of societies. Moral codes, explanations for natural phenomena, and a sense of purpose might have been gifted to early civilizations, shaping their course of development.

The remarkable feats achieved by ancient civilizations in terms of engineering, architecture, and knowledge are considered possible outcomes of exposure to advanced extraterrestrial technology. This perspective challenges the conventional notion that human progress is solely the result of our ingenuity, inviting us to contemplate the potential influence from beyond our world.

Taking this notion a step further, another version of the theory suggests that not just individual belief systems but all religious constructs across cultures were orchestrated by these extraterrestrial beings. In this view, the gods, rituals, and doctrines that have shaped human spiritual practices were deliberately introduced as mechanisms to guide and govern human societies.

Certain conspiracy theories suggest that historical religious figures were alien messengers or emissaries sent to guide humanity's development.

The theory proposes a unified origin for religious narratives and symbols found across cultures. It suggests that the shared themes and similarities could be attributed to this overarching extraterrestrial influence, explaining the remarkable parallels that persist despite geographical and cultural differences.

However, skepticism and criticisms surround this theory. One of the significant challenges lies in the absence of tangible evidence to substantiate claims of ancient extraterrestrial visitations. Interpreting ancient texts and myths can be subjective, influenced by modern perspectives and cultural biases.

Furthermore, the theory may oversimplify the complex factors that contribute to the development of religious beliefs. While intriguing parallels exist among religious narratives, these could also stem from shared human experiences, archetypal themes, and cultural exchanges.

Earth was "seeded" by Aliens

This speculative theory proposes that life on Earth was "seeded" by advanced extraterrestrial civilizations. Imagine aliens deliberately introducing the essential building blocks of life to our planet, initiating the complex process of evolution.

Could it be possible that these alien entities shaped the genetic codes of early life forms, including humans? The theory suggests that their influence might have led to the distinct traits that set us apart from other species.

From a scientific standpoint, this theory often lacks solid empirical evidence and leans heavily on speculation. The intricate origins of life and the intricacies of evolution continue to be studied within established biological and evolutionary frameworks.

Conspiracy theories surrounding UFOs and aliens are as diverse as they are intriguing, often spanning from government cover-ups to secret collaborations with extraterrestrial beings. These theories lack robust evidence and are often speculative; they have captured the imaginations of many. While conspiracy theories can be captivating, they often divert attention from credible scientific research and promote unfounded beliefs.

Chapter 7

Alien Contact and Communications

THE IDEA OF ESTABLISHING contact with beings from beyond our planet has captured the human imagination for generations. It sparks questions about the nature of life elsewhere in the universe, the potential for exchanging knowledge, and the challenges of bridging vast cosmic distances.

Assuming aliens communicate through some form of language or symbolic system, understanding their mode of communication could be incredibly challenging. Our languages and symbols are deeply rooted in human culture and experience, and deciphering an entirely alien system might require a level of abstraction and creativity we can't anticipate.

While the reality of communicating with aliens remains uncertain, the exploration of this idea encourages us to consider our place in the universe and ponder the vast possibilities that lie beyond our planet. It's a reminder of the boundless mysteries that continue to inspire us to reach for the stars.

Crop Circles: Are Aliens Communicating With Us

Crop circles are those mysterious and intricate patterns that appear overnight in farm fields and have held our fascination and curiosity for decades. Coined in the early 1980s, the term "crop circle" describes these enigmatic designs that first gained attention in the countryside of southern England.

However, the origins of this phenomenon trace back even further to a reported incident in England in 1678 known as the "Mowing Devil." The farmer who discovered his crops trampled or cut down in a circular shape attributed it to a devilish entity. Depictions of this event vary, some illustrating a devilish being with a scythe.

Over the years, crop circles have evolved from simple circles to complex formations that encompass geometric shapes, mathematical ratios, and even sacred geometry. Some patterns have been found to incorporate complex mathematical relationships, like the Golden Ratio, a mathematical principle often found in nature and considered aesthetically pleasing. Others reflect shapes and symbols from various religious, spiritual, or even scientific traditions, which indicates an intelligence at work with a deep level of thinking, displaying symbolic or secret designs. These formations can span hundreds of feet and materialize overnight, deepening the mystery of their creation.

Crop circles

(by Agent J., Unsplash)

The question of their origin and purpose remains a topic of heated debate. Various theories have emerged, ranging from natural phenomena like overactive hedgehogs, wind patterns, or electrically charged air currents causing crops to lie down to more elaborate explanations involving the earth's energy fields and meridians. Some believe in extraterrestrial involvement, suggesting that aliens use advanced technology to transmit energy from outer space to create these intricate patterns.

On the other hand, skeptics argue that many crop circles are the result of human hoaxes or artistic endeavors. The easiest way to make them a simple pattern would be with a rope and plank. If one tied a string to a pillar at the center of the circle and worked out from there, then the shape would be symmetrical.

In the present times, the intricate geometric shapes in crop circle creation imply that the circle makers have upgraded their tools from simple planks and ropes to more advanced technological instruments. Possibly, the use of GPS systems has enabled these creators to span vast areas while maintaining the precision of the patterns. They may be using microwaves to flatten large numbers of crop stalks efficiently.

Although proponents advocating for an extraterrestrial origin point out the precision, complexity, and anomalies associated with crop circles as convincing evidence, conclusive proof has not yet been unearthed through investigations.

The concept of crop circles serving as a form of communication from aliens is undeniably captivating. Advocates of this viewpoint underscore the intricate and precise nature of crop circle designs, interpreting them as potential messages from beings beyond our world. They propose that the intricate patterns might encode information or symbols that surpass human capabilities.

Regardless of their ultimate source, it is indisputable that crop circles exhibit both artistic brilliance and symbolic depth. These patterns, in all their various forms, possess an innate beauty and enigmatic quality that consistently captivates people despite their longstanding presence throughout history.

Crop circles have not only fueled debates but have also influenced popular culture. They've been featured in documentaries, films, books, and even fashion and architecture. While skeptics argue that many crop circles can be attributed to human creators, the complexity and scale of certain formations challenge this explanation.

The fascination of crop circles lies in their ability to stir up our imagination and challenge our understanding. They continue to spark wonder, intrigue, and ongoing exploration, whether they're viewed as human artistry or as hints of something beyond our current comprehension.

How to Talk to Aliens

In the scenario of initiating first contact with aliens, mathematics could serve as a unique and universal way to convey complex ideas and establish a basis for understanding. One approach could involve transmitting sequences of numbers, particularly prime numbers, as deliberate signals of intelligent communication. The consistent nature of these sequences could potentially signal our intention to connect.

Furthermore, sharing fundamental mathematical constants like π (pi) or Euler's number could be a way to communicate universal principles that hold true regardless of cultural or biological differences. These constants could act as common reference points, fostering a sense of shared understanding.

A more visual form of communication might involve transmitting geometric patterns or fractals. Recognizable shapes such as triangles or circles could lay the groundwork for mutual comprehension, allowing for the exchange of advanced mathematical concepts without the need for a spoken or written language.

Binary code, a simple mathematical language of ones and zeros, could also play a role. By encoding information in binary sequences, we could potentially convey messages that any civilization with a grasp of binary representation could understand.

Another avenue could involve transmitting basic arithmetic operations and sequences of numbers. This could demonstrate our understanding of mathematical operations and create a platform for further engagement.

Additionally, the use of mathematical equations could help us convey our knowledge of fundamental relationships in physics or geometry. By sharing equations that describe motion or the laws of physics, we might showcase our grasp of the physical world.

While these ideas are intriguing, they depend on several assumptions, such as the aliens' recognition of patterns, their shared understanding of mathematics, and their willingness to respond. It's important to recognize that we're speculating about an unknown civilization's cognitive abilities and communicative methods. Nevertheless, the use of mathematics as a form of communication is a thought-provoking concept that taps into the universal nature of mathematical principles.

"Contact" by Carl Sagan

In Carl Sagan's novel "Contact" and its subsequent film adaptation, the theme of first communication with aliens takes center stage. Dr. Carl Sagan, a renowned astronomer and science communicator, approached the concept of alien communication with a blend of scientific speculation, philosophical contemplation, and the exploration of human emotions. In the novel, the protagonist, Dr. Ellie Arroway, a radio astronomer, detects a series of prime numbers in a radio signal originating from the star Vega. These prime numbers are considered a fundamental mathematical pattern that transcends cultural and linguistic boundaries, making them a plausible choice for extraterrestrial communication.

The prime numbers in the signal suggest an intentional effort to communicate, as they are not typically found in natural cosmic phenomena. This discovery led to global efforts to decode and interpret the message, sparking debates about the nature of the signal and humanity's response.

A team of scientists, including the protagonist, Dr. Ellie Arroway, works tirelessly to decode the message embedded within the signal. The team realizes that the signal contains complex instructions for building a device.

The decoded message provides the blueprints for a machine capable of transporting a single individual to a distant location in space. The device is called the "Machine" and is constructed based on the instructions provided by the extraterrestrial message.Dr. Ellie Arroway becomes the astronaut chosen to travel in the Machine. The journey takes her through a wormhole that transports her to a distant region of space. During her journey, she experiences a sequence of vivid and awe-inspiring visuals.

In the distant region of space, Dr. Arroway encounters an extraterrestrial being in the form of her deceased father. The being explains that they have chosen to communicate through familiar forms to help her understand their message.

Through her encounter with the alien being, Dr. Arroway engages in a conversation that covers a range of philosophical, scientific, and existential topics. The alien being explains that they are part of a vast cosmic community and that the message was intended to convey the importance of knowledge, exploration, and understanding.

Sagan explores the philosophical implications of contact with an advanced civilization, exploring questions about our place in the universe, the nature of faith and science, and the potential for collaboration on a cosmic scale.

He further emphasizes the idea of universality by showcasing the international collaboration required to comprehend the message. Governments, scientists, and individuals from various backgrounds come together in a global endeavor, reflecting humanity's shared curiosity and unity.

Both in the novel and the film, the potential significance of mathematical language as a means of communication is explored. The use of prime numbers serves as a bridge between civilizations, reflecting the belief in the universal nature of mathematics and the possibility of establishing common ground with intelligent extraterrestrial beings.

In "Contact," Sagan combines his expertise in science with his interest in the human condition to create a thought-provoking narrative that examines the profound implications of first contact.

The story raises questions about the nature of reality, the limitations of human perception, and the role of scientific inquiry in exploring the mysteries of the cosmos. It also examines the complexities of understanding, interpretation, and the connections that can arise between disparate civilizations through the medium of mathematics and communication.

Voyager's Golden Disk

Voyager 1 and Voyager 2 are space probes launched by NASA in 1977 as part of the Voyager program. They were designed to explore the outer planets of our solar system and gather data about them. Their main purpose was planetary exploration, involving flybys of Jupiter, Saturn, Uranus, and Neptune.

After completing their planetary missions, the Voyager probes continue their journey to a new phase of their missions that extends far beyond the planets of our solar system into the depths of interstellar space, offering humanity a unique opportunity to explore space beyond the influence of our Sun and to deepen our understanding of the cosmos.

Each of the Voyager probes had a Golden Record Disk. This disk is intended to convey a message of peace, curiosity, and a desire for connection to any intelligent extraterrestrial beings that might encounter the Voyager probes. While the likelihood of the record being discovered by an alien civilization is extremely low, it symbolizes humanity's efforts to reach out and communicate beyond our planet.

The record was developed by a team led by Dr. Carl Sagan, the prominent astronomer who wrote the novel "Contact." The team selected a diverse array of content that would provide insights into the cultural, biological, and technological aspects of Earth.

The "Golden Record" is a gold-plated phonograph record that was included on both spacecraft and contains a curated selection of sounds, music, images, and greetings from Earth, intended to serve as a message to potential extraterrestrial civilizations that might encounter the probes.

The Disks also provide a detailed method on how to read the disk. This was the first and unique attempt by humans to send a message to any intelligent life out there.

The Voyager probes continue their journeys into interstellar space, carrying the Golden Record as a time capsule representing the people of Earth and our place in the universe.

The Search for Intelligent Life

Scientists are always trying to scan the skies to discover any signs of intelligent life anywhere in outer space. To discover such life and to inform them of our presence, the SETI and METI programs were launched.

The SETI (Search for Extraterrestrial Intelligence) and METI (Messaging Extraterrestrial Intelligence) programs are both initiatives aimed at exploring the possibility of detecting or communicating with intelligent extraterrestrial civilizations. While they share similar goals, they differ in their approaches and focuses.

SETI (Search for Extraterrestrial Intelligence)

The SETI program is a scientific initiative with the primary objective of detecting potential signals or indications of intelligent life beyond our planet. Its central goal is to address the intriguing question of whether other intelligent civilizations exist in the universe. This involves actively searching for electromagnetic signals, such as radio waves or laser emissions, that could signify technological activity from extraterrestrial sources.

The SETI program was not started or owned by a single entity but emerged as a concept within the scientific community. The idea of searching for signals from intelligent extraterrestrial civilizations has been explored by various researchers and organizations over the years.

One of the earliest initiatives related to SETI was Project Ozma, conducted by astronomer Frank Drake in 1960. Drake used a radio telescope to listen for radio signals from two nearby stars in the hope of detecting extraterrestrial communications. This project marked one of the earliest attempts to systematically search for signals from intelligent beings beyond Earth.

In subsequent years, the concept of SETI gained interest and momentum within the scientific community. Various organizations and researchers conducted independent SETI projects, often relying on radio telescopes to scan the skies for potential signals.

This work gradually became more organized and collaborative, and the SETI Institute, founded in 1984, is one of the notable organizations dedicated to SETI research. The SETI Institute conducts research, education, and outreach related to the search for extraterrestrial intelligence. It is not a governmental agency but rather a non-profit organization.

The broader SETI community consists of scientists, researchers, and institutions around the world who are interested in exploring the possibility of intelligent life beyond Earth. The community's efforts include utilizing advanced technologies and analyzing vast amounts of data in the quest to detect potential signals.

The SETI is a collaborative and multi-faceted effort within the scientific community. Various organizations and individuals have contributed to SETI research over the years, and the field continues to evolve with advancements in technology and our understanding of the cosmos.

The accomplishments of SETI have not yet yielded a confirmed detection of extraterrestrial signals. However, the absence of such a discovery should not be regarded as a failure, given the vastness of space and the complexities of identifying signals amidst natural cosmic phenomena and human-generated interference.

The challenges facing SETI are considerable. The sheer scale of the universe and the vast distances between stars pose significant hurdles, as the likelihood of detecting a specific signal from a particular source is relatively low. Distinguishing potential extraterrestrial signals from background noise or other sources demands meticulous precision, as false positives could mislead the search. Technological limitations also factor in constraining the sensitivity and range of our instruments. To enhance the prospects of success, advanced technology and extended observation periods are required.

SETI also confronts ethical considerations related to potential contact with extraterrestrial civilizations. The implications of engaging with an alien culture, especially one that might be significantly advanced, pose complex moral questions that warrant careful exploration.

SETI efforts remain active, with various projects searching for potential signals from intelligent extraterrestrial life. These initiatives use radio telescopes to scan the skies for unusual signals that could indicate communication from advanced civilizations.

The Breakthrough Listen Initiative, for example, is using some of the world's most powerful telescopes for comprehensive surveys. The Allen Telescope Array, a collection of radio dishes, continues to be a significant tool for SETI research. Scientists in this field are constantly working on refining signal analysis methods to enhance the accuracy and sensitivity of their searches.

The SETI program's enduring pursuit contributes to our broader understanding of the universe and humanity's place within it. The quest for answers regarding the existence of intelligent life beyond Earth continues to stimulate scientific curiosity and inspire contemplation about our cosmic neighbors.

METI (Messaging Extraterrestrial Intelligence)

The METI program is a venture focused on actively sending intentional messages into space to establish communication with potential extraterrestrial civilizations. Unlike the SETI program, which primarily involves listening for signals from advanced beings, METI involves taking a proactive approach by broadcasting signals ourselves. The fundamental goal of METI is to initiate contact and spark a dialogue with hypothetical intelligent extraterrestrial entities.

The METI program is also a decentralized entity without a single owner. Different researchers and organizations have explored the concept of sending intentional messages to space for potential extraterrestrial recipients.

One notable organization that has been involved in METI-related discussions is METI International. Founded in 2015 by scientists and researchers, including Douglas Vakoch, METI International advocates for transmitting intentional messages to the cosmos as a way to stimulate communication with extraterrestrial civilizations. METI International is one of several entities contributing to the discussion, and the concept of

METI has prompted a range of opinions and ethical considerations within the scientific and space exploration communities.

The concept of METI has been pursued by various individuals and organizations interested in fostering potential interstellar communication. The ownership and initiative behind METI are distributed among those who engage in discussions, research, and potential transmission efforts.

The METI initiative has generated substantial debate and ethical considerations within the scientific community. Advocates argue that sending intentional messages offers us an opportunity to present ourselves to other civilizations, showcasing our curiosity and desire for interaction. They believe that METI could lead to meaningful exchanges of knowledge and ideas that could benefit both humanity and potential extraterrestrial societies.

Critics worry about the potential consequences of attracting the attention of advanced extraterrestrial beings whose intentions, capabilities, and ethical frameworks are unknown to us. Some experts question whether we possess the wisdom to anticipate the outcomes of initiating contact and whether the risks outweigh the potential rewards.

The METI program is characterized by ongoing discussions about its implications, potential success, and possible failures. As of now, there has not been a confirmed case of METI leading to a response from extraterrestrial civilizations. The initiative's success or failure hinges on a range of factors, including the nature of any potential signals sent, the likelihood of them being detected and understood, and the responses they might generate.

Ultimately, the METI program represents humanity's contemplation of our role in the cosmos and our willingness to engage with the unknown. It underscores the complex interplay of scientific exploration, ethical considerations, and the profound mysteries of the universe.

However, there's a division within the scientific community. Some experts and organizations, including those in the SETI realm, are cautious about METI. They raise worries about unforeseeable consequences, potentially drawing attention from unknown or advanced entities.

In the ongoing discussion about whether to actively send messages or solely listen for incoming signals, METI remains a contentious issue. The consideration encompasses scientific, technical, and ethical dimensions.

Scientists have often explored profound themes such as the search for meaning, the potential for communication with other civilizations, and the philosophical implications of encountering advanced beings. The complexities of interpreting communication extraterrestrial brings serious challenges of bridging the gap between human and alien understanding.

Chapter 8

The Fermi Paradox

Where Are All the Aliens?

ON A WARM SUMMER afternoon in 1950, at the Los Alamos National Laboratory. Enrico Fermi, a brilliant physicist known for his wit and insight, was engrossed in a lively discussion with his colleagues at the lunch table. The conversation switched between topics of science, stars, the cosmos, and the mysteries that lie beyond.

Amidst the good humor and good food, there was friendly banter going on with bursts of sudden laughter. With an almost casual air, Fermi leans back and says, "Where is everybody?"

The room falls silent. His colleagues, most of them high-caliber scientists themselves, exchange glances, withdrawn from their chatter by the gravity of his question. Almost everyone understood what he meant in those three simple words. In a blink, Fermi captured the essence of a paradox that has haunted philosophers and scientists for decades. Of course, he was alluding to the issue of why we have not seen any aliens yet, as among billions of star systems, there must be lifeforms that are advanced enough to have found us.

Fermi's question hangs in the air, a beacon of curiosity that pierces through the veil of the unknown. And so, the dramatic scene of Fermi's remark lingers on, a reminder that even the most brilliant minds can be humbled by the mysteries that await beyond the confines of our world and that the quest for knowledge is a journey with no end in sight.

A starry sky seems vast, but all we're looking at is our very local neighborhood. On the very best nights, we can see up to about 2,500 stars, with roughly one hundred millionth of the stars in our galaxy, and almost all of them are less than 1,000 light years away from us or 1 percent of the diameter of the Milky Way.

As many stars as there are in our galaxy, 100 - 400 billion, there are roughly an equal number of galaxies in the observable universe.

The science world isn't in total agreement about what percentage of those stars are "sun-like," which is similar in size, temperature, and luminosity -- Going with the most conservative side of that, say 5 percent, gives us 500 billion sun-like stars. With a very conservative 22 percent potentially habitable Earth-like planet – make a total of 100 billion Earth-like planets.

Let's imagine that after billions of years in existence, 1 percent of Earth-like planets develop life. And imagine that on 1 percent of those planets, life advances to an intelligent level like it did here on Earth. That would mean there were 10 quadrillion, or 10 million billion, intelligent civilizations in the observable universe.

Moving back to just our galaxy and doing the same math and using the lowest estimate for stars in the Milky Way, we'd estimate that there are 1 billion Earth-like planets and 100,000 intelligent civilizations in our galaxy.

Although Fermi's remark wasn't meant to establish a formal paradox, it has since become synonymous with the intriguing question of why, given the vast number of potentially habitable planets in the cosmos, we haven't encountered intelligent extraterrestrial life.

This simple yet thought-provoking question has sparked numerous discussions, theories, and debates about the nature of life, the universe, and the potential obstacles to interstellar communication and contact.

It gets even stranger. Our sun is relatively young in the lifespan of the universe. There are far older stars with far older Earth-like planets, that should have civilizations far more advanced than our own. The technology and knowledge of a civilization only 1,000 years ahead of us could be as shocking to us as our world would be to a medieval person. A civilization

1 million years ahead of us might be as incomprehensible to us as human culture is to chimpanzees.

If a civilization on a planet similar to ours were able to survive for a long time, It would be likely that they would have acquired intergalactic travel technology and would have occupied the multiple galaxy systems.

But the question remains: if there were civilizations scattered across the stars by the billions, why haven't we heard from them? It is from this question that the true paradox was born.

The Milky Way is about 10 billion years old and 100,000 light-years across. If aliens had spaceships that could travel at 1 percent of the speed of light, the galaxy could have already been colonized 1,000 times. Why haven't we heard from any other life?

We have no answer to the Fermi Paradox. The best we can do is "possible explanations." Here are some popular explanations proposed for Fermi's Paradox.

They Are Already Here

Who knows, extraterrestrial aliens are already here and may have integrated themselves into human society, walking among us in plain sight. Your next-door friendly Joe might be from Alpha Centauri star system; all the while, you thought he was from Alaska.

Advanced alien civilizations may have adopted a covert approach to their presence on Earth. Instead of making contact openly, they may be observing and studying humanity, silently coexisting with us to better understand our species and culture. This idea sparks a sense of awe, curiosity, and unrest, prompting us to question if those around us could potentially be extraterrestrial beings.

There are so many unexplained phenomena and probable encounters with UFOs as evidence for this explanation. Proponents suggest that some UFO sightings, mysterious disappearances, or even instances of individuals with extraordinary abilities could be linked to these concealed aliens, subtly influencing our world.

While this explanation may sound like the stuff from horror science fiction, it offers a unique perspective on Fermi's Paradox. It raises thought-provoking questions about the motives and methods of potential extraterrestrial civilizations. Are they here to peacefully coexist, or do they have a more aggressive agenda?

It's essential to approach this explanation with a healthy dose of skepticism, as concrete evidence remains elusive. However, the appeal that we may be sharing our planet with beings from other worlds continues to captivate the imaginations of many.

They Are Watching Us - The Zoo Hypothesis

If flying saucers are real and if they are indeed spacecraft crewed by extraterrestrials, then it resolves many issues immediately. This explanation of Fermi's paradox is the most popular one for the public. It speculates that advanced extraterrestrial civilizations are observing humanity from afar, much like we observe animals in a wildlife sanctuary.

Imagine Earth as a cosmic zoo, where we are the exhibited species under the watchful gaze of alien spectators. These distant observers have intentionally refrained from direct contact, opting instead to observe our planet's natural evolution, societal development, and cultural intricacies from a cosmic vantage point.

Space exploration pioneer Konstantin Tsiolkovsky already discussed this topic decades before Fermi himself. He wrote in 1933 that the extraterrestrials would have no interest in talking to us as we do not want to communicate with wolves, snakes, or gorillas

In 1977, Thomas Kuiper and Mark Morris argued that aliens keep us in quarantine until we can be useful to them in some way. This idea, though scary, continues to occupy the thinking of some scientists.

What can be the motives of these hypothetical extraterrestrial beings? Are they studying us out of scientific curiosity, seeking to understand the nuances of our existence? Or could they be employing a non-interference policy, respecting our autonomy as a species? They may be following the Prime Directive of Star Trek - a policy of non-interference with less-developed life forms.

Supporters of this explanation suggest that UFOs and mysterious encounters with advanced technology could be evidence of this cosmic surveillance. However, concrete proof remains elusive, leaving this explanation as speculative.

They Were Here and Left Evidence of Their Presence

If they are not here at the moment, maybe the advanced extraterrestrial civilizations may have visited Earth in the distant past, leaving behind subtle or not-so-subtle traces of their existence for us to discover.

Various strange artifacts and archaeological mysteries can be viewed as potential evidence of alien visitation. The ancient artifacts, unexplained structures, and even mysterious cave paintings could be remnants of extraterrestrial visits. This explanation makes us wonder, inviting us to reconsider the possibility that our planet's history may have been altered or influenced by the otherworldly visitors.

One compelling example often cited is the perplexing case of the Nazca Lines in Peru. These gigantic geoglyphs, etched into the desert floor thousands of years ago, depict intricate designs that can only be fully appreciated from the far above in the sky.

Some experts think that these lines could have been created as messages or markers for visiting extraterrestrials, suggesting an ancient collaboration between humans and otherworldly beings. Even the Pyramids of Egypt and Stonehenge can be seen as collaborative works of alien beings with humans.

Certain ancient texts and myths from various cultures and religions also supposedly contain subtle accounts of alien encounters. These stories might be the remnants of humanity's interactions with advanced alien visitors.

Nonetheless, the idea that aliens may have visited Earth in the past, leaving behind tantalizing clues, continues to tantalize the imagination of those seeking answers to Fermi's Paradox.

They Are Too Far Away

Milky Way
(by Dennis Degioanni, Unsplash)

There is no doubt about the vastness of the universe and the colossal distances between stars and galaxies. Science fiction movies depict interstellar travel rather easily, and encounters between beings from very different places of origin seem very common. In reality, the speed of light imposes a drastic limitation not only on travel but even on communications, as radio signals cannot travel faster than light.

With the diameter of our galaxy being over 150,000 light years, we have been broadcasting radio signals for just over a century, so our presence could only be detected within a radius of about 100 light-years around the Earth.

A study concluded that only 1% of the galaxy may have already been covered by radio transmissions from different planets and that we will still have to wait about 1,500 years to have a decent chance of being reached by some alien broadcast.

Even if the universe is teeming with intelligent civilizations, the sheer enormity of space and the limitations of the speed of light restrict the ability of extraterrestrial beings to reach us. It would require some advanced yet undiscovered technology and spacecraft in the vast cosmic distances to make interstellar travel possible.

Imagine the star systems may harbor life and civilizations of their own; the distances separating them from one another and our pale blue dot is unimaginably vast.

While our Earth and solar system are relatively young in cosmic terms, the universe itself has existed for billions of years. Extraterrestrial civilizations that may have arisen in the distant past could have already emerged and perished long before we took our first steps into space.

The Great Filter

There's a significant obstacle in the evolution of civilizations that prevents them from progressing to the point of interstellar communication called the 'The Great Filter.'

The concept of the 'Great Filter' is a somewhat bizarre explanation that suggests a significant and mysterious obstacle exists in the path of a civilization's evolution, hindering its progress toward interstellar communication and exploration. This idea may explain the apparent scarcity of advanced extraterrestrial civilizations in the universe.

The key point of the Great Filter explanation lies in the notion that at some point in a civilization's development, there exists a challenging and potentially insurmountable hurdle that significantly reduces the likelihood of its survival or progression.

This hypothetical barrier could be a cataclysmic event, a technological or ethical dilemma, or a combination of factors that ultimately prevent a civilization from advancing to the point of interstellar communication.

And whether we have crossed that 'Filter' or not remains to be answered by the scientists. While the Great Filter explanation doesn't provide a definitive answer to Fermi's Paradox, it points out the complexities of cosmic evolution and the uncertainties in the universe.

They Are Signaling, but We Cannot Recognize their Signal

The advanced extraterrestrial civilizations may indeed be attempting to communicate with us, but the methods they employ are so advanced or unconventional that we have yet to decipher their messages. They may have developed forms of communication that are vastly different from our own. Their signals could manifest in ways beyond our current scientific understanding, utilizing technologies and principles we have not yet discovered or mastered.

The time and space that separates us from these alien civilizations could mean that their attempts at contact occurred in the distant past or are projected into the distant future. Their signals may be operating on timescales that we have not yet comprehended or anticipated.

While this explanation doesn't offer a concrete resolution to Fermi's Paradox, it keeps the possibility open that the aliens may be hailing in ways we have yet to comprehend, and they are awaiting our capacity to decipher their signals and respond.

They Hit the Singularity

Advanced civilizations may reach a point of technological singularity, a state where their technological and scientific capabilities become so advanced that they surpass our current understanding.

The technological singularity is a hypothetical future point in time when artificial intelligence (AI) and machine intelligence surpass human intelligence and capabilities. It envisions a moment when AI systems become so advanced that they can improve and enhance themselves at an exponential rate, leading to rapid and potentially transformative changes in society. This could result in unprecedented technological advancements, while others express concerns about the ethical and societal implications of such a scenario and humans becoming slaves to AI.

Artificial Intelligence created by the aliens may have surpassed their own intelligence. In such a scenario, these civilizations may have achieved feats we can scarcely comprehend, including potentially transcending physical limitations and possibly transforming into entities that are no longer confined to traditional forms of communication or exploration. As a result, they might exist in a dimension or state beyond our current capacity to perceive or interact with.

Such a development may even lead to their self-destruction. This underscores the fragility of advanced civilizations and how even the most technologically advanced societies may be vulnerable to their own undoing.

The Universe is Here for Us

Or maybe the simplest explanation is true. Earth and humanity hold a unique and privileged position in the universe, and there are no other advanced civilizations out there. This solution solves Fermi's Paradox completely.

When thinking about the existence of alien life, we often consider that there are many "difficult steps" toward the development of intelligent life. such as the evolution of multicellular organisms, the emergence of life itself, and the development of symbolic language. Each of these milestones is pivotal in a civilization's journey.

The quest for extraterrestrial intelligence goes beyond just finding life; it's about understanding the diverse paths civilizations might take in their technological evolution.

By exploring these ideas, we gain insight into the potential challenges and achievements of life beyond Earth, enriching our perspective on the vastness and complexity of the universe.

The concept also raises questions about the nature of the universe itself. Is it an exclusively human-centric creation designed specifically for our existence? Such a proposition challenges the principles of cosmology and the laws of physics that govern the cosmos, suggesting a level of cosmic intentionality that has yet to be demonstrated scientifically.

It is important to acknowledge that our understanding of the universe is continually evolving. While the search for extraterrestrial intelligence has not yielded conclusive evidence of other civilizations, it remains an active and ongoing pursuit.In the spirit of scientific exploration, it's prudent to remain open to the possibility of extraterrestrial life. The vastness and diversity of the cosmos invite us to consider the potential existence of intelligent beings elsewhere, fostering a sense of wonder and humility in the face of the universe's mysteries.

The concept that the universe is exclusively for humanity is a viewpoint that remains speculative. Are we alone in the universe? The question remains unanswered as yet.

Consciousness is Not Inevitable

While the universe may harbor countless planets capable of supporting life, the development of conscious, self-aware beings is not guaranteed and may indeed be a rare occurrence.

At the heart of this explanation lies the notion that consciousness, particularly in the form we humans experience, is a complex and highly specific outcome of evolution. It may depend on a multitude of factors, including the precise combination of genetic, environmental, and evolutionary processes. These factors would need to align in a particular way to produce beings with self-awareness, intelligence, and the ability to ponder the cosmos.

If consciousness is not an inevitable result of evolution, then many potentially habitable planets might have life, but it could exist in simpler forms, lacking the capacity for complex cognition and self-reflection. In such cases, these life forms would be unlikely to develop advanced technology or engage in interstellar communication.

Consciousness, undoubtedly a defining aspect of life's richness, bestows upon us the capacity to engage in a wide array of tasks, making it invaluable in our intricate, modern world. However, when we consider the process of evolution, it becomes apparent that it operates without foresight. This leads us to question how consciousness could have provided an advantage to our ancestors, who were struggling to survive in the African landscape some 50,000 years ago.

One might argue that consciousness could have been a distinct disadvantage in their circumstances. For instance, when faced with the immediate threat of a prowling lion, the most advantageous response would have been swift action—running to safety—rather than pausing to contemplate the grace of these big cats as they stalked their prey.

While consciousness undoubtedly enriches our lives today, the evolutionary advantages it offered to early humans in survival situations, such as evading predators, may not have been immediately apparent. This intriguing paradox prompts us to explore the intricate relationship between consciousness and the evolution of our species, shedding light on the complex interplay between our cognitive abilities and the challenges of our ancestral environment.

This perspective challenges our assumptions about the prevalence of intelligent life in the universe. It suggests that even if conditions for life are common, the emergence of conscious beings like us may be rare, making us a cosmic rarity rather than the norm.

They are Non-Biological Life

This offers a fascinating perspective on Fermi's Paradox, suggesting that intelligent life in the universe may not be carbon-based like us and, as a result, may not be easily detectable by our current methods and assumptions.

Life as we know it on Earth is carbon-based, relying on organic chemistry and water as the foundation for biological processes. However, the universe is vast and diverse, and it's entirely plausible that alternative forms of life have emerged elsewhere based on different elements, chemistries, and biochemistries.

Non-biological life could exist in forms we can't readily comprehend. These life forms might not require water or carbon-based molecules, and their biology and biochemistry might be radically different from what we're familiar with. Consequently, our traditional methods for detecting life, such as searching for organic molecules or water, may not be suitable for identifying these exotic life forms.

Moreover, non-biological intelligence might not communicate in ways that are recognizable to us. They may utilize forms of communication, technology, or energy that are entirely foreign to our understanding.

Consequently, we could be surrounded by non-biological intelligence without realizing it, as our methods for detecting and communicating with them may not align with their modes of existence.

The Occam's Razor

All of these explanations highlight the complexity of the Fermi Paradox and the wide range of possibilities that could contribute to the absence of contact with extraterrestrial civilizations. It's a fascinating topic that continues to spark speculation and debate among scientists and thinkers.

To narrow down on a single explanation, we may turn to Occam's razor. It is a philosophical concept that suggests when you have many possible answers to a question, the simplest one is often the best. It's like saying that if you hear hoofbeats, think of horses, not zebras or giraffes.

This means we shouldn't make things more complicated than they need to be, and we should choose the easiest explanation that makes sense. It helps scientists and thinkers make good decisions and solve problems more easily.

Occam's razor applied to Fermi's Paradox suggests that we should consider the simplest explanation for the lack of contact with extraterrestrial civilizations, such as practical limitations or the possibility that civilizations may have come and gone. Complex and exotic theories should be considered only after we have exhausted exploring these straightforward possibilities.

Chapter 9

The Psychological Impact of Alien Abductions

Dr. John Edward Mack

HE WAS A MEDICAL doctor, writer, and professor of psychiatry. He served as the head of the Department of Psychiatry at Harvard Medical School from 1977 to 2004. He won the Pulitzer Prize for his remarkable book "A Prince of Our Disorder: The Life of T. E. Lawrence."

Dr. Mack was a clinical expert in child psychology, adolescent psychology, and the psychology of religion. He was also known as a leading researcher on issues related to teenage issues, such as suicide and drug addiction. He later undertook serious research into the psychology of human abduction by aliens.

Dr. Mack initiated a psychological study of around 200 people who reported encounters with aliens in the early 1990s that lasted over 10 years. He presented his findings in numerous papers, articles, and interviews and wrote a book entitled "Abduction." Dr. Mack is probably the most acclaimed and professionally qualified academic to have studied the subject of human abduction by aliens and talked about it.

His findings were so shocking that in an unprecedented move, the Harward University Management ordered a committee of peers to confidentially review Dr. Mack's clinical investigation of the people who had shared their alien encounters with him. It was the first time in Harvard's history that a tenured professor was subjected to such an investigation to ascertain whether his actions were professionally responsible or not.

After over a year of investigation, Harvard University issued a statement that endorsed Dr. Mack's academic liberty to study as he desired and to express his opinions freely and that Dr. Mack remains a member in good standing of the Harvard Faculty of Medicine.

In an unexpected turn of events, on September 27, 2004, while he was in London to deliver a lecture at a conference, he was walking back to his hotel after having dinner with friends when he was struck by a vehicle. He was seriously injured, lost consciousness at the scene of the crash, and was pronounced dead shortly afterward. He was 74. The driver was arrested, convicted of drunk driving, and jailed for 6 months.

Interview with Dr. Mack

Dr. John Mack, in an interview with PBS, said some very disturbing things about alien abduction. Dr. Mack was no quack doctor; he was the Head of Psychiatry at none other than the prestigious Harvard Medical School. What he said was remarkable in many ways. Perhaps it was the first time a leading medical doctor with impeccable credentials talked about alien abductions. There may be no one more qualified to talk about the subject.

When initially confronted with the phenomenon of alien abduction, Dr. John Mack found it difficult to take it seriously. Raised with the belief that contact with extraterrestrial intelligence, if ever, would occur through radio communication, he was skeptical of the idea that beings from another outer space could enter our world and have physical and emotional interactions with human beings.

Despite his initial skepticism, Dr. Mack diligently investigated the matter, seeking to rule out other explanations, such as psychosis or fabricated stories. He was struck by the consistency, sincerity, and emotional impact of the abductees' stories, leading him to reluctantly acknowledge the phenomenon as a genuine mystery.

He noted that abduction experiences often occurred in a state of full consciousness of the victims, not in dreamlike states. Abductees described encounters where they were paralyzed by blue light or energy, removed from their surroundings, and subjected to various surgical procedures by these beings, including probing and the removal of reproductive material in an attempt to create hybrid offspring.

Dr. Mack highlighted that these experiences were not limited to Western culture but were a global phenomenon occurring in indigenous communities and various other countries worldwide.

He emphasized five key factors that any theory about this phenomenon must account for: the consistency of the stories, the absence of a plausible experiential basis and lack of any mental illness history of the victims, the presence of physical evidence like cuts and lesions, the connection to UFO sightings with abductions, and the occurrence of abductions in children as young as two years old.

Dr. Mack clarified that his perspective wasn't based on belief but on extensive clinical work and ruling out alternative explanations. He also noted that those with significant stakes in society, such as job positions, were often hesitant to admit to their abduction experiences due to potential threats to their employment; this includes airline pilots who had witnessed UFOs up close and have kept quiet.

Dr. Mack's research and observations led him to view alien abduction experiences as a perplexing and widespread phenomenon deserving of serious consideration and investigation. The following material is extracted from his book "Abductions."

Alien Abduction Experience – A Psychological Perspective

Many abductees often recall a series of encounters rather than just a single dramatic incident. These experiences typically begin in early childhood or even infancy. Signs of childhood abductions include memories of the presence of small beings in the bedroom, unexplained intense light, a humming or vibratory sensation, instances of floating down hallways or out of the house, close-up sightings of UFOs, horrifying dreams of being taken into stark operating rooms for intrusive medical procedures, and time lapses of an hour or more where parents couldn't find the child. Common indicators for both children and adults include waking up paralyzed, a sense of dread, and the presence of strange beings in the room.

In some cases, these alien beings are remembered as friendly playmates or even healers. Abductees have reported being cured of life-threatening illnesses by these beings. Initially, abductees often view the aliens as protectors during early childhood, but the encounters become more serious and disturbing as they approach puberty.

Interestingly, abduction experiences seem to have a familial pattern, spanning three or more generations. Parents who have had close-up UFO sightings or abduction experiences may initially deny their encounters and those of their children, possibly to avoid revisiting their own abduction traumas. Occasionally, children may report seeing a parent on the alien ship, but when confronted, the parent may not recall the experience.

Three Classes of UFO Phenomenon

The first level deals with literal, physical phenomena connected to UFO sightings. This includes visual and radar spotting of UFOs, light and sound associated with them, burnt patches of earth, lesions or implants on abductees, and more. These events can be studied using Western empirical methods. Ufology initially focused on these tangible occurrences until the concept of the abduction syndrome emerged.

The second level encompasses phenomena that might be understood within our current understanding of space and time, given advanced scientific and technological knowledge. This might mean extraterrestrial technologies that are much more advanced than ours. Examples include spacecraft propulsion systems, their rapid movements, the mysterious way aliens seem to pass through solid barriers, memory and consciousness manipulation, and the creation of alien-human hybrids. While we don't grasp the intricacies of these phenomena yet, future developments in sciences like physics or biology might elucidate them.

The third level goes into experiences and phenomena that defy our current understanding of space and time. Abductees report things like thought travel, the feeling that their experiences exist outside of our conventional understanding of space and time, the consciousness of other vast realities, a strong connection to cosmic consciousness, and dual human/alien identities. Additionally, there's the notion of aliens being able to change shapes, sometimes first appearing as animals or UFOs disguised as familiar objects. These experiences don't align with scientific principles and our current belief systems.

How Do Abductions Begin?

Abduction encounters typically begin in various settings, with homes and automobiles being the most common. They can also happen while walking in nature or even at school yards for children. The onset of abduction is often marked by unusual signs like intense blue or white lights filling the room, strange buzzing or humming sounds, an unexplained presence, or the direct sighting of humanoid beings and their spacecraft.

These experiences sometimes start during the night or early morning, and initially, the abductee may mistake them for dreams. However, upon closer examination, it becomes clear that they were fully awake during the events. The abductee may feel a mixture of shock and sadness when realizing that what they perceived as a dream was a bizarre and recurring experience they can't explain.

During the abduction, abductees frequently report a subtle shift in consciousness, which feels as real or even more so than their usual state. They often describe being "floated" through walls, windows, or the roof of a car, with a slight vibratory sensation. The beings accompanying them guide them to a waiting spacecraft, and abductees typically discover they have been numbed or paralyzed by a touch from these beings. While they can often move their heads and see what's happening, they may choose to close their eyes to avoid confronting the terrifying reality of the situation.

The spacecraft associated with these abductions vary in size, from a few feet to several hundred yards wide, and have silvery or metallic exteriors in a cigar, saucer, or dome shape. Bright white, blue, orange, or red lights emit from the craft's bottom and porthole-like openings. Abductees are initially taken into a smaller craft, which may then ascend to a larger "mother" ship. Sometimes, they are lifted directly to the larger ship, with a view of the ground or house below receding dramatically. Abductees may attempt to resist or stop the experience, sparking a debate within abduction research about whether these encounters can be halted and whether doing so is advisable.

Independent Witnessing

While there are instances of independent witnesses to abductions, they are relatively infrequent, and the evidence, though compelling, can be subtle and hard to prove conclusively. Often, spouses of abductees are "switched off" during the event, seemingly in a state deeper than sleep, even appearing lifeless. This can lead to abductee frustration, especially when attempts to wake the partner, even by screaming, prove unsuccessful.

Inside The Alien Crafts

Abductees often describe being transported into UFOs through the bottom or side portals. Inside, they usually find themselves in a dimly lit room before being moved to brighter, larger spaces for various procedures. These rooms have curved walls and ceilings, are brightly lit, and contain unfamiliar equipment. The interiors feel sterile, similar to hospitals.

Inside the ships, abductees encounter various types of alien beings. The most frequently reported are the "grays" – small, humanoid creatures standing three to four feet tall. These "grays" come in two main types: the shorter, drone-like workers and a taller "leader" or "doctor" figure. Abductees sometimes identify these beings by gender, not based on physical appearance, but on an intuitive feeling. The grays have distinct features like large, black, almond-shaped eyes that many abductees find unsettling to look directly into. They often wear single-piece garments with occasional cowls or hoods.

The leader figure, slightly taller than the worker grays, seems older and is always in control of the procedures on the ship. Abductees often have complex feelings towards this being, sometimes recognizing them from multiple encounters and feeling both a bond and resentment.

Communication with these aliens is experienced as telepathic, eliminating the need for a shared language.

Surgical Procedures

The abductees typically find themselves undressed and placed on a body-fitting table where most of the procedures take place. They may undergo these experiences alone or witness other individuals undergoing similar examinations. The alien beings closely examine the abductees, giving them a sense that their thoughts have been fully understood and even influenced. Various instruments are employed to collect samples from the body, including skin, hair, and internal tissues.

These instruments are used to penetrate nearly every part of the abductees' bodies, ranging from the head to the genitalia. Some describe extensive procedures within the head, which they believe could potentially alter their nervous systems.

The most prevalent and significant procedures revolve around the reproductive system. Instruments are utilized to collect sperm samples from males and manipulate or fertilize the eggs of females. Abductees often recount experiences of being impregnated by alien beings and later having hybrid pregnancies terminated. They witness the placement of fetuses in containers on the ships and observe incubators where hybrid babies are nurtured. On occasion, they encounter older hybrid individuals, including children, adolescents, and adults, whom they intuitively recognize as their own.

These encounters evoke profound distress in abductees, initially causing intense fear, although reassurances from the aliens that no significant harm will befall them and the use of anxiety-reducing or anesthesia-like methods may alleviate some of their distress.

These methods impact the body's "energy" or "vibrations," diminishing fear and pain and inducing states of relaxation. However, in certain cases, these techniques are only partially effective, allowing intense emotions like terror, pain, and anger to emerge.

The physical and biological aspect of abduction experiences appears to involve genetic or quasi-genetic engineering aimed at generating human-alien hybrid offspring. While there is no conclusive evidence of aliens inducing genetic changes in a strictly biological sense, this possibility remains open.

The Alteration of Consciousness

The abduction process involves not only physical procedures but also involves a profound alteration of the abductees' consciousness. This transformation extends beyond mere cognitive processes, going deeply into their emotional and spiritual realms, fundamentally reshaping their perceptions of themselves, the world, and humanity's role within it. This information is primarily conveyed through direct telepathic communication between the abductees and the alien beings, as well as through powerful visual images displayed on television monitor-like screens aboard the ships.

The abductees often start receiving this information during childhood or adolescence, but its full significance becomes clear only much later in life, often with the assistance of investigators. These messages contain disturbing scenes depicting an Earth devastated by a nuclear holocaust, lifeless polluted landscapes, and catastrophic natural disasters, which the abductees interpret as prophetic visions of the planet's future. Some abductees are even given specific roles in this apocalyptic scenario, such as feeding survivors or being relocated to participate in the evolution of life in the universe.

Some abduction researchers believe that these images may not be shown to positively alter the planet's course but rather to study the abductees' reactions and deceive them into believing the aliens care about Earth's fate while secretly planning to take over the planet. They argue that if the aliens genuinely cared about humanity's well-being, they would intervene more directly in our affairs to improve the situation.

The aliens' response to these concerns, as reported by abductees, suggests that they believe humanity is not ready to acknowledge their existence and would react aggressively toward them. They claim that their methods differ, aiming to bring about change through a shift in human consciousness rather than coercion.

Upon their return to Earth, abductees typically have varying degrees of recollection of the abduction. Sometimes, they remember it as a dream, while other times, they wake up with unexplained cuts, lesions, lumps under the skin, headaches, nosebleeds, or missing garments or jewelry. Fatigue is a common post-abduction experience, as if they've been through a stressful ordeal.

Physical Aspects of Abduction

The physical aspects associated with abductions serve primarily to corroborate the abduction experiences themselves, as their effects are subtle and wouldn't, by themselves, convince a well-trained clinician of their significance. For instance, the cuts, scars, scoop marks, and small fresh ulcers that appear on abductees' bodies after their experiences are usually too minor to be medically significant.

Similarly, abductees often believe they have been pregnant and had the pregnancy removed during an abduction, but these occurrences are challenging to prove or verify.

Electrical or electronic devices, such as TVs, radios, watches, clocks, and lights, are reported to malfunction in connection with abductions or when abductees are nearby. However, establishing a direct link between these disturbances and the abduction process is nearly impossible.

Abductees commonly believe that some kind of homing object has been inserted into their bodies, particularly in the head and other body parts, allowing the aliens to track or monitor them, akin to tracking animals with various devices. These alleged implants may be felt as small nodules beneath the skin, and in some instances, tiny objects have been recovered and subjected to biochemical and electron microscopy analysis.

Notably, there's no conclusive evidence that the recovered implants are composed of rare or uncommon materials. Determining the nature of an unknown substance without additional information about its origin is a formidable challenge. Even if these objects were indeed left in the human body by alien beings, it would be virtually impossible to prove, and the aliens could have adapted the objects to human biology, making them appear unremarkable under analysis.

The Pathology of Abduction

Abductions are profoundly impactful experiences that can both traumatize and transform those who go through them. These encounters are traumatic in several ways. First, the actual experiences involve being paralyzed and taken against one's will by unfamiliar beings who subject individuals to invasive and often degrading procedures. Understandably, this is deeply disturbing.

Second, abductees often grapple with a persistent sense of isolation and estrangement from the people around them. They may feel different, like they don't quite belong in society, even if they outwardly appear to be functioning well.

Third, abductees undergo what can be termed as "ontological shock" as they come to terms with the reality of their encounters. Raised in a world where the idea of intelligent beings breaching Earth's boundaries is considered highly unlikely, they often cling to the hope of finding a psychological explanation for their experiences, even when they know deep down that what happened was as real as any conversation.

Lastly, the traumas associated with abductions are unique in that they can occur at any time without a discernible pattern. Unlike many other traumas that have a finite duration, abductions can resurface unpredictably throughout an individual's life. This can be particularly distressing for parent abductees who become aware that their children are also having abduction encounters, leading them to confront their own buried experiences to support their children.

In addition to these long-term traumatic effects, abductees may suffer from various subtle but persistent symptoms related to their abduction experiences. These can include fears such as a fear of hospitals and needles, as well as physical symptoms like headaches, sinus issues, body pains, abdominal, urological, and gynecological issues, and disruptions in sexual functioning. Interestingly, some abductees have reported instances of healing for various conditions following their encounters, adding a layer of complexity to their experiences.

Perceptual Transformations

One of the most significant aspects of the abduction phenomenon is the evolving relationship between abductees and the alien beings. Initially, this relationship may have been playful and intimate, especially in early childhood. However, as puberty approaches and the reproductive hybrid "project" begins, it tends to shift towards a more disturbing and traumatic dynamic. Abductees may start to feel like victims, viewed coldly by the aliens or treated merely as specimens in the aliens' project, leading to a sense of betrayal.

Yet, as the abductees search deeper into their experiences and acknowledge the extraordinary nature of their encounters, something profound happens. The initially frightening and adversarial relationship seems to transform into a more reciprocal one, fostering increased communication between humans and aliens. Abductees may even develop a profound love for the alien beings, sometimes surpassing the love experienced in human relationships, and believe that this love is reciprocated. The connection through eye contact plays a crucial role in this transformation. Despite initial resentment about their genetic material being used in the hybridization project, abductees may eventually perceive themselves as participants in a process with value for the creation and evolution of life.

Some may argue that this shift is a defensive mechanism or self-delusion, a way for the ego to retain a sense of control or to balance the emotional cost of a traumatic experience with positive contributions to the universe. Alternatively, it could be that facing the shattering experience of abduction opens abductees to transpersonal meaning, universal love, and connectedness, enabling them to feel compassion.

In the realm of transformational and spiritual growth related to abduction experiences, it's challenging to pinpoint cause and effect. Does an abductee's openness to the possibility of past lives lead to the emergence of past-life memories, or does the emergence of such memories, facilitated by therapeutic work, expand their personal horizons and connection to universal consciousness?

Furthermore, categorizing the alien beings as purely good or deceptive and hostile may not capture the complexity of their interactions with abductees. The idea of light beings being inherently good and caring while grays are seen as indifferent or businesslike might oversimplify the intricate nature of interspecies or inter-dimensional relationships, which may not adhere to human-like polarizations or categories.

Chapter 10

Beyond Earth's Horizon

HUMANS HAVE A STRONG desire for space travel due to their curiosity, the drive for exploration, scientific discovery, and the human spirit. Space travel represents an ambitious and ultimate inspirational pursuit that pushes the boundaries of human capability and fosters a deeper understanding of the universe.

The idea of humans venturing out into space to visit extraterrestrial civilizations or explore distant planets, rather than waiting for aliens to come to us, is an exciting idea. We have waited long enough. Either we are alone in the universe, or the extraterrestrials are too far away. Exploring the unknown, expanding knowledge, and finding new worlds are rooted in the human spirit.

Science fiction has explored the idea of humans traveling to new worlds and encountering alien civilizations for many years. Authors like Jules Verne, H.G. Wells, Isaac Asimov, Arthur C. Clarke, and countless others have crafted imaginative stories that take readers on journeys to distant planets and galaxies. These works of fiction have not only entertained us but have also sparked scientific and technological innovations, as well as discussions about the possibilities and challenges of space exploration.

How to Talk to Aliens

Who knows when we might encounter an alien from far above? How will we interact with such an entity? Experts are curious and think about this intriguing topic of communicating with intelligent extraterrestrial beings.

They speculate whether we could understand their language and how we might achieve this.

Some experts express optimism about our ability to communicate with aliens and argue that there could be a universal grammar shared among Earth's languages. They suggest that this universal grammar might extend to extraterrestrial languages, particularly in terms of syntax.

On the other hand, some experts take a more pessimistic view. They speculate that aliens, if they even have brains, might perceive and conceptualize their world in ways that are entirely foreign to us, making their language and thought processes a mystery.

This skepticism appears justified given our ongoing struggles to understand intelligent species on our own planet, like dolphins, despite our genetic proximity to them. The vast gulf between us and an alien species would likely present even greater challenges.

One proposed solution often discussed is using mathematics as a universal language, which was used on the Voyager Golden Record, a message intended for potential extraterrestrial recipients. But even this could cause misunderstandings, and even a well-intentioned message designed to represent Earth's culture could be misinterpreted by aliens due to their lack of cultural context.

No one knows how best to mathematically convey our ideas, emotions, and feelings. While mathematics might serve as a starting point for long-distance communication, it would likely fall short of conveying the depth of human emotions. Language, despite its complications and potential for misunderstandings, offers a greater potential for expressing feelings. Ultimately, the question of how to communicate with aliens remains unanswered, and we find ourselves with more questions than answers

Communicating With Alien Visitors

Science fiction often comes to the rescue to resolve such dilemmas. In the 2016 movie "Arrival," a linguist is shown as she struggles to communicate with visiting aliens. Communication with the extraterrestrial beings is portrayed to be a complex and grinding process in the movie.

The movie follows the story of Dr. Louise Banks, a linguist played by Amy Adams, who is recruited by the U.S. government to help decipher the language of the aliens. These aliens are mysterious and enigmatic, resembling giant cephalopods with seven tentacle-like limbs. They arrive on Earth in an enormous, floating spacecraft, and their purpose is initially unknown.

Dr. Banks begins by attempting to understand the basics of the alien written language, which consists of intricate circular symbols called logograms. Unlike human languages, the alien language is non-linear, with the ability to convey complex ideas and concepts simultaneously. As Dr. Banks goes deeper into deciphering the logograms, she realizes that understanding their language is intimately connected to understanding their perception of time, which is non-linear as well.

Throughout the movie, Dr. Banks and her team make gradual progress in their efforts to communicate with the aliens. They establish a rudimentary form of communication, starting with simple exchanges and progressing to more advanced conversations. Dr. Banks learns to think in a non-linear fashion, allowing her to perceive events and experiences from her past and future simultaneously, mirroring the aliens' perspective.

The breakthrough in communication comes when Dr. Banks and the aliens exchange crucial information that could potentially prevent a global crisis. This exchange of knowledge highlights the power of language as a tool for bridging the gap between two entirely different species and for fostering mutual understanding.

"Arrival" explores profound themes of language, time, and the nature of communication, making it a thought-provoking and emotionally resonant science fiction film. How communication is established with the aliens serves as a central element in the narrative, emphasizing the importance of linguistic and cultural understanding in our interactions with the unknown.

Where No One Has Gone Before

The mission of the Starship Enterprise in the Star Trek TV series is "to explore new worlds, seek out new life and civilizations, and boldly go where no one has gone before." Captain James T. Kirk, Captain Jean-Luc Picard, and their respective crews are tasked with representing the United Federation of Planets in a peaceful and diplomatic mission as they travel through the universe. The Star Trek is primarily set in the future, ranging from the mid-22nd century to the late 24th century.

They conduct scientific research, establish diplomatic relations, and provide assistance to those in need, all while upholding the principles of the Federation, which include promoting peace, cooperation, and the betterment of all sentient beings. The Enterprise serves as a symbol of hope, exploration, and unity in the vastness of space.

Star Trek holds a special place in the hearts of fans for several compelling reasons. It offers an optimistic glimpse into the future, envisioning a world where humanity has overcome its divisions and works together to explore the vastness of space. This hopeful outlook provides a refreshing contrast to the often dystopian narratives found in other science fiction movies.

Such science fiction movies also serve as a catalyst for projecting the future into reality by inspiring innovation, fostering visionary thinking, initiating ethical discussions, and addressing current societal issues in futuristic contexts. It anticipates challenges and risks associated with emerging technologies, stimulates interest in space exploration, and has even directly influenced technological development.

Star Trek is about the spirit of exploration and discovery, appealing to our innate curiosity about the unknown. It ignites our desire to venture into uncharted territories, whether that's in the depths of space or within ourselves.

It introduced innovative technologies that have had a significant impact on the real world. For instance, the communicator, resembling modern flip phones, and the tablet-like machine predicted the development of tablet computers. The Warp drive, the tele-transporters, the Holodeck, and cloaking technology are fantasy now but may develop into realities.

The series distinguishes itself through its diverse and imaginative portrayal of alien species, ranging from humanoid to non-humanoid forms, each characterized by unique cultures and values. These alien species serve as a platform for exploring themes of multiculturalism, diplomacy, and social commentary while also providing complex and relatable characters like Spock.

Interactions between humans and aliens are central to the series, fostering narratives that emphasize tolerance, understanding, and the potential for cooperation across species. The series' commitment to creativity, makeup, and costume design has resulted in iconic and memorable alien races, contributing to its enduring appeal and cultural impact.

The Prime Directive in Star Trek, known as Starfleet General Order 1, is a central ethical principle guiding Starfleet personnel to avoid interfering in the internal affairs of other civilizations, especially those less technologically advanced, to preserve their cultural integrity and natural development. This directive raises profound moral and ethical dilemmas as it mandates non-interference even in situations where intervention might alleviate suffering or injustice. It underscores respect for cultural diversity and self-determination while serving as a recurring theme that prompts exploration of complex ethical questions and the consequences of well-intentioned interference, thereby challenging viewers to reflect on the balance between help and autonomy in interstellar diplomacy.

Star Trek has inspired scientists and engineers to pursue careers in space exploration and technology development. Concepts from the series have influenced real-world space research and engineering projects.

Star Trek's timeless appeal transcends generations. Its themes of exploration, cooperation, and the boundless potential of the human spirit continue to resonate with audiences of all ages, ensuring its enduring status as a cultural phenomenon that continues to inspire and captivate.

Major Issues Hindering Space Travel

Space travel, whether within our solar system or to distant stars, presents an array of practical and technological challenges that stretch the limits of human ingenuity and perseverance.

One of the most daunting aspects of space travel is the sheer scale of the distances involved. The cosmos is unimaginably vast, and even missions within our solar system can take years to plan and execute. For interstellar travel, the distances are on a scale that boggles the mind, requiring not just advanced technology but also a fundamental shift in our approach to exploration.

Time is another formidable challenge in space travel. Even with the most cutting-edge propulsion systems, journeys to the nearest stars would only happen across generations. This introduces a host of logistical, psychological, and generational hurdles. How do you sustain a mission that your grandchildren may see through to completion? How do you motivate generations of explorers to embark on a journey that they will never personally complete?

One of the key technologies that requires massive improvements for space travel is propulsion. Traditional chemical rockets, while effective for missions within our solar system, are simply not up to the task of interstellar travel. Achieving the velocities needed for such journeys requires entirely new propulsion technologies. Concepts like ion drives and nuclear propulsion show promise, but they bring their own set of challenges, from energy generation to resource management.

The sustainability of long-duration missions is a paramount concern. On a spacecraft, everything must be recycled, from air to water to food. The closed-loop ecosystems required for such sustainability are complex and demanding. Waste management, resource utilization, and the preservation of crew health over extended periods all require innovative solutions.

Radiation exposure is another major issue for the survival of human beings. Space is a harsh environment filled with harmful radiation, including cosmic rays and solar radiation. Prolonged exposure can damage biological tissues and spacecraft electronics. Developing effective shielding and countermeasures is an ongoing challenge.

Navigating and communicating over vast distances in space is no small feat. Precise positioning and communication with Earth or other spacecraft are essential for the success of any mission. Additionally, for interstellar travel, entirely new navigation paradigms would need to be developed to account for the colossal distances and the fact that traditional navigation markers like stars would change over time.

The health effects of extended space travel are also a concern. Astronauts on long-duration missions can experience muscle and bone loss, cardiovascular issues, and radiation-related risks. Developing countermeasures and medical treatments to mitigate these effects is essential.

Interstellar travel introduces an even bigger set of challenges beyond those encountered in our solar system. These challenges include the need for self-sustaining ecosystems on spacecraft, managing the long-term psychological effects on crew members, and ensuring the ability to repair or replace critical systems during journeys that span generations.

Space travel comes with environmental and ethical considerations. The debris left in Earth's orbit and the potential contamination of celestial bodies raise environmental concerns. Ethical questions about how to handle potential extraterrestrial life, if encountered, are also a challenge.

The cost and funding of space travel, especially interstellar missions, are significant obstacles. Securing the necessary financial resources and maintaining public support for such endeavors over the course of decades or centuries is a formidable challenge in itself.

Addressing these multifaceted practical and technological difficulties in space travel requires a harmonious blend of scientific research, engineering innovation, international collaboration, and unwavering commitment. While the challenges are formidable, the relentless pursuit of knowledge and the indomitable human spirit continue to push the boundaries of what is achievable in our quest to explore and understand the cosmos.

Sleeping While You Space Travel

Hibernation technology is particularly relevant for missions involving extremely long-distance space travel, where traditional awake and alert astronauts face numerous challenges related to resource consumption, radiation exposure, and psychological well-being. By lowering their metabolic rates and resource needs, hibernation could potentially extend the feasibility of such missions. In the state of hibernation, the astronauts will sleep during their journey. Hibernation and its issues in space travel are very aptly portrayed in the 2016 science fiction movie "Passengers" starring Jennifer Lawrence.

The fundamental principle behind hibernation technology is to significantly lower the metabolic rate of astronauts. This entails slowing down vital bodily functions such as heart rate, respiration, and metabolism. Doing so would dramatically reduce the body's energy requirements, oxygen consumption, and food intake.

Achieving this state of reduced metabolic activity would likely require medical intervention. Astronauts would receive carefully controlled treatments, possibly involving drugs or therapies, to induce and maintain the hibernation-like state. The process would need to be reversible, allowing astronauts to awaken when required.

While in hibernation, astronauts would still require a minimal level of life support to ensure their well-being. This would include a controlled environment with regulated temperature, humidity, and oxygen levels. Systems for waste removal and recycling would also be necessary to manage bodily waste products.

Since astronauts would remain in a suspended animation-like state, their nutritional and hydration needs would be significantly reduced. They might receive essential nutrients intravenously or through other controlled methods to sustain their health during the journey.

Continuous monitoring of the astronauts' vital signs and overall health would be crucial to ensure their well-being throughout the hibernation period. Safety protocols and fail-safe mechanisms would also be essential to address any potential complications or malfunctions.

It's important to note that while hibernation technology is a fascinating concept, it remains largely speculative and has not been realized in practice for human space travel. Significant research and development would be necessary to address the numerous technical, medical, and ethical challenges associated with implementing such a system.

Can Humans Colonize Space?

Human colonization of space is a concept that has captivated the imaginations of scientists, science fiction writers, and enthusiasts for many years. While the idea is technically feasible, it comes with an array of formidable challenges. These challenges span from developing advanced life support systems capable of sustaining human life in the harsh environment of space to finding effective ways to protect colonists from the harmful effects of cosmic radiation.

One of the most frequently discussed targets for colonization is Mars. Its relative proximity to Earth and the presence of some resources like water and ice make it a logical choice. However, even establishing a sustainable colony on Mars requires meticulous planning and substantial infrastructure development. It involves creating habitats capable of withstanding the planet's extreme temperatures and dust storms, as well as generating food and water locally.

International collaboration will likely play a pivotal role in any large-scale space colonization effort. The success of the International Space Station (ISS) has demonstrated the benefits of international cooperation in space exploration. A joint effort would not only pool resources and expertise but also share the responsibilities and costs associated with such ambitious projects.

Technological advancements are indispensable in making space colonization a reality. The development of more efficient propulsion systems could significantly reduce travel times and costs. Resource utilization, such as mining asteroids for essential materials, could provide the raw materials needed for building and sustaining space colonies. Artificial gravity solutions are necessary for mitigating the adverse health effects of long-term space habitation.

Economic viability is another critical factor. Space colonization would require substantial financial investments. Public and private sectors would need to collaborate, and space activities that generate revenue, like asteroid mining or space tourism, could play a crucial role in funding these endeavors.

Moreover, space colonization is not a short-term project. It demands a commitment that spans generations. The challenges will evolve, and solutions will need to adapt to changing conditions. Continuous research and development, along with a dedication to overcoming obstacles, will be essential.

While the idea of human colonization of space is both exciting and promising, it remains an ambitious and complex endeavor. Nonetheless, with the right combination of technological innovation, international collaboration, financial investment, and ethical responsibility, it represents a potential path for humanity's future beyond Earth, with the potential to open new frontiers of exploration and existence.

... and the Journey Continues

This was an extraordinary journey through the enigmatic world of aliens and UFOs. You may be left with a profound sense of awe and curiosity. The tales of unexplained aerial phenomena and encounters with unidentified flying objects have ignited our imaginations and challenged our perceptions like never before. The promise of contact with intelligent beings from beyond our world lingers in the air, a tantalizing notion that stirs the soul.

Yet, a healthy skepticism remains. It is a reminder that while the search for truth in the skies is an ongoing quest, it is a complex and enigmatic journey, one that requires discernment and patience.

As this final chapter concludes, it invites you to reflect on the mysteries that still elude our understanding and the enduring human quest to explore the unknown. The truth about UFOs remains an enigma, but the journey to uncover it continues, fueled by a blend of wonder and skepticism that defines our exploration of the cosmos.

Epilogue

A Journey from Skepticism to Belief

As I CLOSE THESE pages about UFOs and aliens, I find myself standing at a point I never expected. When I first embarked upon this journey, I viewed the world of unidentified flying objects and extraterrestrial encounters with a skeptic's eye. The tales of bright lights, mysterious craft, and abductions seemed, at best, a collection of misconceptions or, at worst, a plethora of fake stories to gain notoriety for financial gains.

When I was in the early stages of researching and writing this book, I approached the subject with a scientific, critical eye, questioning the credibility of countless sightings and abduction accounts. I harbored doubts, as many do, about the validity of these claims. I questioned whether the stories were products of misidentifications, psychological delusions, or simply hoaxes perpetuated by attention-seekers.

However, as I researched deeper, reading the abductees' accounts, scrutinizing evidence, and weighing the testimonies of both skeptics and believers alike, my thinking began to shift. The vastness of the accounts, the patterns that emerged, and the often profound impact on the lives of those who experienced these phenomena began to soften my skepticism. I found myself questioning not the veracity of the witnesses but the limits of my understanding.

Certainly, not every UFO sighting can be attributed to extraterrestrial visitors; many can be explained by natural phenomena, classified military projects, or optical illusions. But there remains a significant portion of cases that defy all conventional understanding, pushing us to reconsider what we think we know about our universe and our place within it.

Abductions, perhaps the most controversial of all UFO-related phenomena, also proved to be a profound challenge. While it's easy to dismiss such stories as fabrications, results of psychological disorders, or hallucinations, doing so ignores the depth and consistency of experiences shared by people from diverse backgrounds, cultures, and age groups. Many of these individuals had nothing to gain and often much to lose by sharing their stories.

I was sobered by the sincere and emotional narratives of individuals who had reported abduction experiences. Their accounts, while often shrouded in mystery, conveyed a sense of genuine shock and bewilderment that could not be easily disregarded. I began to understand the trauma of their experiences and the profound impact they had on their lives.

The UFO phenomenon challenges our assumptions about the nature of reality, the scope of human knowledge, and the possibilities that exist beyond the boundaries of our terrestrial existence.

I believe in the need for continued rigorous investigation, scientific inquiry, and open-minded discourse on the subject. I believe in the importance of respecting the experiences and perspectives of those who have encountered the unexplained. And I believe that the UFO phenomenon, whatever its ultimate nature, serves as a testament to the enduring human spirit of curiosity and exploration.

So, where does this leave me? I can no longer dismiss the UFO phenomenon as mere fiction or fraud. While I cannot say with certainty what lies behind every mysterious light in the sky or every unexplained experience, I am now convinced that we are not alone in this universe – and that our understanding of reality might be more complex than we ever imagined.

This book does not provide you with definite answers, but it should leave you with an open mind and a deeper sense of wonder as you look up at the starry night sky. Whether you are a skeptic, a believer, or somewhere in between, I hope this exploration has encouraged you, as it has for me, to these phenomena with renewed curiosity and an open mind. The universe is vast, and our journey of understanding has only just begun.

Thank you for staying with me on this extraordinary journey.

References

Stephen Webb, "If the Universe Is Teeming with Aliens . . . Where Is Everybody?, Springer, 2015

John E. Mack, "Abduction-Human Encounters With Aliens", Ballantine Books, New York, 1995

Nick Redfern, "Top secret Alien Abduction Files", Disinformation Books, 2018

Kevin D. Randle, " The Government UfO Files: The Conspiracy Of Cover-Up", Visible Ink Press,2014.

"2022 Annual Report on Unidentified Aerial Phenomena", Office of The Director of National Intelligence

"Preliminary Assessment: Unidentified Aerial Phenomena". Office Of The Director Of National Intelligence, 25 June 2021

J. Allen Hynek "Hynek UFO Report", MUFON, 2020

S. Friedman and K.Marden, "Captured! The Betty And Barney Hill UFO Experience", The Career Press, 2007

www.ingramcontent.com/pod-product-compliance
Lightning Source LLC
Chambersburg PA
CBHW070723130626
46553CB00005B/2122